CAMBRIDGE LIBRARY COLLECTION

Books of enduring scholarly value

History

The books reissued in this series include accounts of historical events and movements by eye-witnesses and contemporaries, as well as landmark studies that assembled significant source materials or developed new historiographical methods. The series includes work in social, political and military history on a wide range of periods and regions, giving modern scholars ready access to influential publications of the past.

The History of the English Electoral Law in the Middle Ages

The introduction, during the Middle Ages, of a representative system into English political life, was an event of great historical significance, and has since been central to academic debate. Written by Ludwig Riess (1861–1928), an eminent twentieth-century historian, this pioneering account of the medieval English electorate profoundly influenced the study of English constitutional history, as it questioned the fundamental assumptions of the scholarship that preceded it. First published in German in 1885, it critically evaluated the aims of the elected representatives, and re-assessed the general electoral regulations of the period. In so doing, it provided new solutions to some problems encountered by previous scholars, such as defining parliamentary boroughs, and accounting for the rise of a national representative assembly. First translated into English in 1940 by K. L. Wood-Legh, this controversial and seminal work remains highly relevant to legal scholars and historians today.

T0382580

Cambridge University Press has long been a pioneer in the reissuing of out-of-print titles from its own backlist, producing digital reprints of books that are still sought after by scholars and students but could not be reprinted economically using traditional technology. The Cambridge Library Collection extends this activity to a wider range of books which are still of importance to researchers and professionals, either for the source material they contain, or as landmarks in the history of their academic discipline.

Drawing from the world-renowned collections in the Cambridge University Library, and guided by the advice of experts in each subject area, Cambridge University Press is using state-of-the-art scanning machines in its own Printing House to capture the content of each book selected for inclusion. The files are processed to give a consistently clear, crisp image, and the books finished to the high quality standard for which the Press is recognised around the world. The latest print-on-demand technology ensures that the books will remain available indefinitely, and that orders for single or multiple copies can quickly be supplied.

The Cambridge Library Collection will bring back to life books of enduring scholarly value (including out-of-copyright works originally issued by other publishers) across a wide range of disciplines in the humanities and social sciences and in science and technology.

The History of the English Electoral Law in the Middle Ages

Ludwig Riess

CAMBRIDGE
UNIVERSITY PRESS

CAMBRIDGE UNIVERSITY PRESS

Cambridge, New York, Melbourne, Madrid, Cape Town,
Singapore, São Paolo, Delhi, Tokyo, Mexico City

Published in the United States of America by Cambridge University Press, New York

www.cambridge.org
Information on this title: www.cambridge.org/9781108010696

© in this compilation Cambridge University Press 2011

This edition first published 1940
This digitally printed version 2011

ISBN 978-1-108-01069-6 Paperback

THE HISTORY OF THE
ENGLISH ELECTORAL LAW
IN THE MIDDLE AGES

CAMBRIDGE
UNIVERSITY PRESS
LONDON: BENTLEY HOUSE
NEW YORK, TORONTO, BOMBAY
CALCUTTA, MADRAS: MACMILLAN
TOKYO: MARUZEN COMPANY LTD

THE HISTORY OF THE
ENGLISH ELECTORAL LAW
IN THE MIDDLE AGES

by

LUDWIG RIESS

Translated with additional notes
by

K. L. WOOD-LEGH

M.A. McGill, B.Litt. Oxon., Ph.D. Cantab.

CAMBRIDGE

AT THE UNIVERSITY PRESS

1940

PRINTED IN GREAT BRITAIN

CONTENTS

INTRODUCTION

ALITTLE over fifty years ago, in 1885, the book that is here translated was first published. Its author was a young German scholar who in the previous year had obtained the degree of Dr.Phil. from Berlin University for a thesis comprising the first four chapters of the present volume. In interest and importance, however, Riess's work far surpassed the average essay of this kind, and ever since its appearance it has profoundly influenced the study of English Constitutional History.

At the time when Riess undertook his researches the leading authorities on this subject were Stubbs in England and Gneist in Germany. The great works which we owe to these men were based on careful study, but the length of the periods they covered often precluded the investigation of details by the authors themselves, and there were practically no monographs dealing with particular points which could supplement their own researches. Moreover, these scholars could not fail to be influenced by the preconceptions of their age—preconceptions inherited from the constitutional struggles of earlier centuries and strengthened by the new power and prestige to which, in their own life-time, Parliament had attained.

Thus it was needful that the work of the great authorities should be subjected to the critical examination of younger scholars prepared to question even the fundamental hypotheses on which their elders had built, and it was further necessary that those who undertook this examination should follow a new method, and instead of writing chronological histories of the constitution during long periods, should choose particular points or problems, making each the subject of minute investigation.

The first scholar of his generation possessing the necessary critical faculties who approached English Constitutional History in this way was the young Ludwig Riess. He took as the subject of his monograph, mediaeval parliamentary elections, some aspects of which had previously been discussed, though in a far less scholarly way, by Cox. In preparing his work he seems to have examined minutely all the relevant material that was then available in print (manuscript sources being inaccessible to him, as he appears not to have been able to visit England until after his book was published), and having been led by his researches to conclusions far different from those then generally accepted, he set forth his views with a youthful enthusiasm and an air of certainty that often approach to arrogance.

What these views were and wherein they differed from those of Riess's older contemporaries will be made sufficiently clear in the book itself. Also the place of the work in the literature of English Constitutional History has already been adequately explained by Mr G. T. Lapsley[1] and need not be recapitulated here. Suffice it to say that many of the points on which Riess pronounced with assurance are still controversial, and that whatever may be thought as to the correctness of Riess's theories they cannot be disregarded.

It has therefore seemed desirable that the *Geschichte des Wahlrechts* should be translated into English, and the fact that for the last ten years the book has been out of print leads me to hope that the present translation may also serve as a new edition for those who cannot now obtain the original.

But to publish a translation of this book without verifying the references or calling attention to errors would be misleading. I have, therefore, endeavoured to check all the references, a task which has not been easy, since very many of the page numbers proved to be incorrect. I have, however, succeeded in tracing almost all of them, and where the mistake has been only the giving of an incorrect page number or some similar slip, I have made the correction without indicating that there has been any change. Errors of fact or points which subsequent research has further elucidated have been dealt with in additional footnotes, but in preparing these, I have tried to confine myself to what seemed strictly necessary lest the work of Riess himself should be obscured by over much comment.

One section of the book, however, has not been reproduced. This is the main part of Chapter V, covering pages 76 to 86

---

[1] Preface to R. G. D. Laffan's translation of Pasquet's *Essay on the Origins of the House of Commons*.

of the original, where an attempt is made to explain the changes in English economic and social life during the fourteenth century. But Riess was never an economic historian, and the views of older scholars, especially Erwin Nasse, on which he depended have been almost entirely abandoned as a result of more recent research. The section is, therefore, of practically no value and as it has little bearing on the main argument of the book, I have, on the advice of Professor Postan and Mr J. Saltmarsh, decided to omit it.

A number of friends have assisted in the preparation of this volume. My thanks are especially due to Mr G. T. Lapsley of Trinity College, Cambridge, who, besides being always ready to advise, very kindly read over the manuscript, making many suggestions by which the work has benefited. Mr J. G. Edwards of Jesus College, Oxford, at whose suggestion the translation was originally undertaken, has given me valuable advice on a number of difficult points.

To my father I am indebted for constant help, especially in the wearisome task of verifying Riess's many references, and to my aunt, Miss L. S. Stevenson, for assistance in preparing the index.

K. L. W.-L.

CAMBRIDGE

July 1939

PREFACE

THE INTRODUCTION of the representative system into the mediaeval English constitution is an act of universal historical significance and therefore it has repeatedly been made the subject of research by German as well as by English scholars. Recently an eminent English historian has described the rise of the lower house and the formation of the franchise with somewhat greater coherence and in minute detail; and has thereby won the reputation of having surpassed all his predecessors. Nevertheless, as this English scholar himself admits, most essential problems, such as the definition of parliamentary boroughs and the active franchise, remain altogether obscure.

Thus, frequently as they have already been discussed, it may be permissible to present the results of a new investigation of these questions. The present work, therefore, is concerned in the first place with the causes of the rise of a national representative assembly in England, and then with the franchise and its development in the Middle Ages. I dedicate it to the man who, of all my university teachers, has done most to lead me to understand the methods of research of the school of Ranke, and to think objectively, Dr Hans Delbrück.

THE AUTHOR

BERLIN
10 *August* 1884

A HISTORY OF
ELECTORAL LAW IN ENGLAND
DURING THE MIDDLE AGES

CHAPTER I

The AIM and TASKS of the ASSEMBLY of
ELECTED REPRESENTATIVES

A LMOST every year since 1295 an assembly of elected representatives of the country has been summoned by Edward I and his successors. Everyone knows what importance this elected parliament attained in the course of time; and how (though not indeed until our own century) the majority of civilized states have adopted the English representative system. In the political life of the peoples the parliamentary franchise is of the greatest value; its exercise has been attended with far-reaching consequences for the development of the nations.

But by these circumstances we are only the more impelled to enquire with the greatest possible diligence and freedom from preconceptions, with what intentions, in the distant Middle Ages, the institution of the lower house was first created in Britain; what duties were to have been incumbent on the commons, and actually were imposed, which made their coming together necessary to the state.[1] For the conditions of those distant times are not shown in a clear light by the mere repetition of the oft-quoted passage from a writ of summons to one of the first parliaments of Edward I; "as the most just law established by the wisdom of sacred princes exhorts and firmly enjoins that *what concerns all shall be approved by all* so it is very

---

[1] It is, in my opinion, fatal for Cox (*Antient Parliamentary Elections*) that, in spite of his many digressions, he has not had this question at all in mind, and in his antiquarian researches has been guided almost entirely by the conceptions and prejudices of our century.

evident that common dangers should be opposed by common means ".[1] Ranke was the first to quote this passage;[2] and then Cox ventured to draw far-reaching conclusions from the wording.[3] Stubbs, who found in the Theodosian Code the true source of these words, which indeed at the first glance betray themselves as borrowed, nevertheless sees in them the essence of Edward I's political principles.[4] But from a writ addressed to the spiritual magnates which an ecclesiastical chancery official composed with unctious raptures and ornamented with foreign ideas, it is impossible to discover the motives that induced Edward I to create the lower house;[5] moreover, the italicized words were used only in a superficial comparison, and their application is much restricted by the main clause.[6]

[1] "Sicuti lex justissima provida circumspectione sacrorum principum stabilita hortatur et statuit, ut, quod omnes tangit, ab omnibus approbetur, sic et innuit evidenter, ut communibus periculis per remedia provisa communiter obvietur" (P.W. I, 30).

[2] Englische Geschichte, I, 85.   [3] Antient Parliamentary Elections, p. 74.

[4] Constitutional History, II, 5, 128. Further (p. 249), this passage has obviously misled him to the conclusion that Edward I was probably more concerned to have the assent of the commons to the main outlines of his policy than to be in accord with his kingdom with regard to taxation and legislation. "The principle etc." [Stubbs rightly states that the passage comes from the Code of Justinian, not Theodosius. An attempt to vindicate Stubbs's interpretation has been made by P. S. Leicht ("Un principio politico medioevale", in Reale Accademia Nazionale dei Lincei, Rendiconti, XXIX, 232 ff.). This, Mr G. T. Lapsley has discussed and criticized in his Additional Notes to Laffan's translation of Pasquet's Origins of the House of Commons, App. III, note O.]

[5] [Recent research has shown that the phrase quod omnes tangit, ab omnibus approbetur, frequently occurs in ecclesiastical documents of the thirteenth century to express the principle of the need of the clergy's consent to taxation (see M. V. Clarke, Medieval Representation and Consent, pp. 264–6). Consequently its appearance in the writ summoning the ecclesiastics to the parliament of 1295 may have been a concession to clerical opinion. It had, of course, nothing to do with the rights of the lay commons. Mr J. E. A. Jolliffe (Constitutional History, p. 349) regards this dictum as "an effort to convince the archbishop and his suffragans that further aid for the relief of Gascony, which Edward suspected would be refused on the ground that the clergy were not concerned, was really in their own interest". See Stubbs, Select Charters, p. 480: "Res vespa maxime sicut ceterorum regni ejusdem concivium agitur in hac parte: your interests are equally involved with those of the rest of the realm in this affair." Edward had tried to establish this sense of common interest in a writ to the archbishop of York of the previous year—quos communiter negocium istud tangit—but without as yet suggesting the corollary of securing the approval of all concerned (Parliamentary Writs, I, 25).]

[6] Gneist (Englische Verfassungsgeschichte, p. 359) therefore takes up only the words of the conclusion "to meet common danger with means taken in common".

It must be admitted that modern scholars have inferred from the indefinite wording of the introduction to this writ that, for the common affairs of the state, a supreme council of the king was to be created on the broadest possible basis, only because to us, in our century, this idea is so near and so congenial.

In the English revolts of the thirteenth century, the creation of a body of elected representatives which should take part in the government was never an aim or a demand of the insurgents; so it could not occur to a victorious and popular king to set up so complicated and costly an institution, or even to summon it at ordinary times, merely in order to deliberate with all touching what concerned all.[1] Rather the forces which, in mediaeval England, led to the establishment of an elected assembly as an element in the constitution of the country were really the following.

I

The kings lacked effective control over the conduct in office of the sheriffs, who in accordance with Norman methods of government, originally administered their shires with very wide powers. Indeed, great kings had early sought to obviate the dangers to the royal power which this position of the officials in the counties constituted. They had reduced the authority of the sheriffs by taking from them the higher judicial functions and entrusting these to itinerant judges; and by raising smaller districts that were united in the hands of a single lord, or were inhabited as towns, to the position of Liberties, within which the sheriff, without special authorization from the king, had no right of interference for police purposes.[2] But neither for the subjects nor for the crown were these measures altogether adequate; one of them, moreover, if widely applied, must bring with it the danger of tearing the country into atoms, and create difficulties of all kinds.

---

[1] For a long time to come, moreover, the activities of the commons in no way correspond to such high intentions.

[2] "Ingressum non habeo in libertatem illam" is said in countless reports from the sheriffs to the chancery; see Merewether and Stephens, *History of Boroughs*, I, 343. [The existence of Liberties certainly lessened the sheriffs' power, but it is doubtful whether this was ever a motive for their creation, since the lords of Liberties were usually less amenable to the royal authority than were the sheriffs.]

In the long contests which the monarchy had to maintain against the barons, it became very apparent how greatly the common opposition was inflamed and embittered by the oppressions of the sheriffs. Indeed, an important part of Magna Carta, the provisional treaty between king and people, is directed precisely against the arbitrary conduct and ruthless severity of the highest county officials.[1]

In order not to allow this inflammable material for new quarrels to accumulate too much, Henry III, as early as 1226, thought it prudent to pacify the threatening discords between his subjects and the sheriffs by a royal decision.[2] He chose the form of causing four of the more lawful and discreet knights (" de legalioribus et discretioribus militibus "), elected by each of the disturbed counties, to attend an assembly of the barons at Lincoln.

With true insight Edward I recognized this danger and the necessity of securing, to some extent, both his subjects and the crown against the encroachments of the sheriffs and their officers. This tendency of his home policy can be traced in many and important measures. In two ordinances of 1285 he threatened with severe punishments those sheriffs who either through false statements in their returns, or through carelessness, left him ill-informed.[3] In 1293 he arranged that the complaints that were brought in excessive numbers to him and his baronial parliament should nevertheless be answered conscientiously and without delay.[4] Finally, and most important of all, after 1295, he called upon the communities of his subjects themselves to inform him concerning the administration of his provinces, and the oppressions committed by his officials; he established the delegation of commissions from the administrative districts to the central government as a permanent institution in English constitutional life.

[1] Merewether and Stephens were the first rightly to apprehend this. *History of Boroughs*, I, 429: "...sheriffs and bailiffs, to restrain whose oppressions and exactions was a material object of the charter."

[2] "ad terminandas contentiones ortas inter quosdam vicecomites nostros et homines comitatuum suorum super quibusdam articulis contentis in carta libertatis eis concessae" is said in the writs to the sheriffs (*Report on the Dignity of a Peer*, Appendix I, p. 4).

[3] *Statutes of the Realm*, I, 90, 91, xxxix.

[4] The order concerning this is printed by Stubbs, *Constitutional History*, II, 263, n. 2.

At first sight it may perhaps appear rash to seek to derive this particular idea from the course of development and from the trend of thought of the great king. But from every side it is apparent that it was just this tendency that was dominant, precisely this need that prevailed in mediaeval England.

The very extensive use of the new institution for voicing complaints against the county officials can itself serve as a proof, so considerable is the number of charges against the sheriffs; so regularly were immediate remedies or at least thorough investigations ordered.[1] Moreover, for a long time to come, other measures contain indications that the three Plantagenet Edwards recognized, above all, the unity of interest of crown and people against the officials as was seen in no other fiscal administration of the Middle Ages. The king limited the authority of the sheriffs no further;[2] but he rendered possible effectual control based on close observation and thus provided for the full accountability of his officers. It was ordained that the sheriffs should allow the reports which they sent into chancery to be inspected and sealed by those who wished to do so; persons to whom this was denied had only to complain.[3]

According to a decree of 1315, only such men should be made sheriffs as held in their own right (not from great lords) land sufficient whereby they could be held to answer to the king and people.[4] Then in 1346 it was laid down that the sheriffs should

[1] For examples see Rot. Parl. I, 48, 32; 164, 44; 195, 25; 289, 5; 291, 14; 372, 11; II, 9, 21; 38, 37; 40, 47, etc.

[2] [This seems to take no account of the justices of the peace, the development of whose office in the course of the fourteenth century resulted in a great diminution of the sheriffs' authority. His power and importance were also lessened by the practice of appointing special collectors of the subsidies granted in parliament. See Maitland, Constitutional History, pp. 233–4, and J. F. Willard, Parliamentary Taxes on Personal Property, 1290 to 1334, Cambridge, Mass. 1934.]   [3] Rot. Parl. I, 295, 7.

[4] Rot. Parl. I, 353, 5. Repeated, II, 8, 15. [Here there is a conflation of two passages in the text. All land was held of some lord and no attempt was made to prescribe of whom the sheriffs should hold their lands. All that the statute required was that the sheriffs should have sufficient land in the counties they administered, and that they should not be stewards or bailiffs of the great lords, since such employment would interfere with the discharge of their duties as sheriffs. "Et que nul soit Visconte s'il ne eit terre suffisaunt-ment en meisme le Counte ou il serra Visconte, por respondre au Roi et au Poeple: Et que nul qui soit Seneschal ou Baillif de graunt Seigneur soit fait Visconte, s'il ne se ouste d'autri Service, mes tiel le soit qui del tout peusse entendre a l'office du Visconte faire por le Roi et por le Poeple" (Rot. Parl. I, 353).]

be suitable men, possessing land, and inhabiting the county committed to them, and should always be appointed for only one year.[1] Moreover, special commissions were sent into the counties "to hear and determine the oppressions and other offences committed by the sheriffs and other ministers of the king".[2]

While in these measures the general endeavour of the king as well as of the people to supervise the conduct of the officials is proved, we have also express statements in the statutes and records from the feudal period which describe the provision of security for the subjects as the principal, and even as the only, cause of the summoning of representatives of the country.

In the preamble to the statute of 5 Edward II, it is said that "since many persons are oppressed by the ministers of the king and without a common parliament no remedy for such grievances can be found, we ordain that the king shall hold a parliament once or twice in every year".[3] Substantially the same is said in 30 Edward III: "for the maintenance of the said articles and to amend diverse mischiefs and grievances that arise from day to

---

[1] *Rot. Parl.* II, 161, 22. This was again enjoined in 1372; see II, 313, 33. [Riess exaggerates the community of interests between the king and his subjects with regard to the sheriffs. The demand that they should be annually appointed first occurs in the "Provisions of Oxford" (Stubbs, *Select Charters*, p. 391). It was the subject of several Commons' petitions in the fourteenth century, but though these were granted and the annual appointment prescribed by statute (*Statutes of the Realm*, I, 283, vii), it was only very slowly that the practice of keeping sheriffs in office for longer periods was abandoned.

The requirement that the sheriffs should be residents of the counties they administered was also purely in the interest of the subjects. It too first appears in the "Provisions of Oxford"; and in the Commons' petitions it was usually joined to the requests for annually appointed sheriffs. On the whole, it seems to have been earlier complied with, as the great majority of the sheriffs appointed in the fourteenth century held lands in the counties committed to them, which, from the point of view of mediaeval administration, constituted residence.]

[2] "De oppressionibus et aliis gravaminibus per Vicecomites et alios Ministros Regis factis audiendis et determinandis" (*P.W.* II, ii, 260, 7 (17 August 1324)). E.g. an investigation of this kind concerning Thomas de Newebriggyne, clericus, in London is extant (*P.W.* II, ii, Appendix, 246–7, 107).

[3] *Statutes of the Realm*, I, 165, 29: "Pur ceo qe...auxint mulz des genz grevez par les ministres le Roi encontre dreitur, des quels grevances homme purra avoir recoverir sans comun parlement; nous ordenons qe le Roy tiegne parlement une foitz par an ou deux foitz, si mestre soit...."

day let parliament be held every year ".[1] In 50 Edward III it was specified as a duty of parliament "to redress errors and wrongs in the kingdom if any are found ".[2] In like manner, all "good and lawful" persons were in 5 Edward III invited by the king and council to bring complaints of the abuses of the sheriffs and their officers.[3]

I am, of course, far from assuming that with the summoning of the commons a new right of complaint was created for the subject. Previously also every Englishman who thought himself wronged, or any community which was discontented with its administration, could appeal to the help and decision of the highest court. But with the commons, the machinery, so to speak, was created for bringing such complaints from individuals as well as from communities to the place where they would be decided, before the king and his great council, *Magnum Concilium*. For this purpose no one except the governed themselves could determine the executive commission; only with elected representatives could it be hoped that friction in the administrative machinery might be entirely removed.[4]

II

Again, the extent to which parliamentary representatives were bound to take an active part in the business of local government has not been recognized.

They were, probably, regularly employed to convey to the petitioners the answers to the petitions which they had brought

[1] *Statutes of the Realm*, I, 374, 10: "Item pour meintenance des ditz articles et estatutz et redresser diverses meschiefs et grevances qui veignent de jour en autre, soit parlement tenuz chezcun an...."
[2] *Rot. Parl.* II, 355, 186: "de faire corrections en Roialme des Erroures & Fauxtees, si nuls y soient trovez".
[3] *Rot. Parl.* II, 60, 21.
[4] [One of the most recent writers on parliamentary history emphatically denies the view set forth in this section, saying that "the king never summoned them [the knights and burgesses] especially to hear their petitions,... it was the business of the subject to approach the monarch for this purpose, not the monarch to summon the subject". He further cites some evidence to show that "The growing custom of using the meetings of parliament to approach the king for remedies was, indeed, clearly unwelcome to Edward I: 'Pur ceo ke la gent ke venent al parlement le Roy sunt sovent deslaez et desturbez a grant grevance de eus e de la curt par la multitude des peticions ke sunt botez devant le Rey'." B. Wilkinson, *Studies in the Constitutional History of the Thirteenth and Fourteenth Centuries*, p. 21.]

with them,[1] and to bring back to the sheriffs or burgesses in their counties other ordinances or advice which the king wished to make known;[2] but far more than this, important official duties and business of state, not only for their own but also for other counties, were wont to be committed to them.

To be a collector of taxes in a wide district is certainly an unpleasant and difficult task. We are, therefore, the more surprised to find in the lists of those appointed collectors and assessors the names of men who in the same year had represented their shire or their borough. Immediately after the representation of the country had been introduced this principle clearly appeared.

On 6 October 1297 a parliament was opened; on 14 October the collectors of the tax to be imposed were already assigned. There we find Robert de Barry and Almaric de Noers appointed as collectors of the tax in Buckinghamshire; when we examine the corresponding election return, it appears that both of them were present in this very parliament as members for Buckinghamshire. Likewise we meet at least one of the representatives of Berkshire, Suffolk, Bedfordshire, Essex, Middlesex, Surrey, Southampton, and Lincolnshire again in the list of collectors.[3]

More precise information with regard to the duties of such commissioners is yielded by the surviving instructions of 1316. There it is said that the collectors of each district shall undertake the collection "together with a clerk whom they shall choose for this purpose according to their discretion, and for whom they will be surety". One half of the amount due they should deliver by 3 November 1316, the other by 17 April 1317. And to this wearisome and difficult office were appointed, on 5 August 1316 —three days before the close of parliament—the two representatives of Lincolnshire, Huntingdonshire, and so forth, and one of the members from numerous counties—Surrey, Derby, Essex, Kent, Buckingham, etc.[4]

[1] "...Et fust dit as Communes, Il plest au Roi, que ces qui voleient demurer pur attendre & avoir Respons de lour Petitions,...." (*Rot. Parl.* II, 316, 7 (47 Edward III)).
[2] *Rot. Parl.* II, 119a, 11 (14 Edward III). It was ordained that "nientmeyns soit meisme l'assent mys en fourme patente soutz le Grant Seal d'Engleterre, et liveretz as Chivalers des Counties, de reporter en lour pais".
[3] *Parliamentary Writs*, I, 64. On 23 October an order was issued to them to collect also a ninth from the boroughs and ancient demesne.
[4] *P.W.* II, ii, 167.

The members, moreover, had to undertake this duty even for other counties. Thus, in 1316, Nicholas de Kingston represented Wiltshire, but was a collector for Gloucestershire, etc. Similarly, in 1296, Robert de Berkele was a member for Gloucestershire, but collector for Herefordshire, and it appears that the like is true of all his colleagues.[1]

It is, therefore, not surprising that, in the time of Edward III, all the members united to pray the king to free them from this obligation. In the year 1352: "pray all the knights, citizens and burgesses who have come to this parliament for the counties, that none of them be made a collector of the tax which is granted in this parliament to our lord the king".[2] But significant enough was the emphatic refusal to this: "Il semble au Conseil que ceste Petition n'est pas resonable."[3]

So, then, a main reason for having the country represented was, in the view of the central government, to commit this important business of the financial administration to those who

[1] *P.W.* I, 54. [The tax here referred to was that of July 1297. It was granted by an irregular assembly, containing no elected representatives of shires or boroughs, which cannot be described as a parliament. The men appointed to assess and collect this subsidy in almost every county were residents, not of that county, but of some neighbouring shire, which was in each case specified. (See J. F. Willard, *Parliamentary Taxes on Personal Property*, 1290 to 1334, p. 16.) This, Riess misunderstood, and assumed that the counties of which the men are said to be were those they had represented in parliament.

The genuine cases in which men were appointed to collect subsidies in counties other than those they had represented in parliament are few, and it is probable that the men so employed held lands in both counties. Thus Roger de Baskerville, who in 1306 was knight of the shire for Hereford (*Return of Members of Parliament*, I, 21) and in the same year was appointed a collector of the subsidy in Shropshire, is shown by an Inquisition Post Mortem of 13 Edward I to have inherited lands in both these counties (*Cal. of Inquisition Post Mortem*, II, 355).

Again, in 1307 Roger de Engelfeld represented Berkshire and was a collector of the subsidy in Oxfordshire (*Return of Members of Parliament*, I, 27). I have not been able to discover what lands he held at the time, but an acknowledgement of debt which he made in 1313 shows him to have been then possessed of lands in both counties (*Cal. Close Rolls*, 1313–18, p. 215), and it is more likely that these lands were already his before 1307 than that he acquired them in the intervening period.]

[2] *Rot. Parl.* II, 240, 27: "Item, Prient touz les Chivalers, Citezeins et Burgeis, qi sont venuz a cel Parlement pur les Countees, que nul de eux soit fait Coillour de l'Eide a fire Seigneur le Roi ore a cest Parlement grante."

[3] This petition, still repeated in vain in 1373, was eventually, in 1377, granted by the old and feeble Edward III (*Rot. Parl.* II, 368, 48). But, at least, the commons remained bound, before their departure for home, to designate suitable collectors and assessors (*Rot. Parl.* III, 66, 51 (2 Richard II)).

had been elected, or, at any rate, to trustworthy persons, and to supply them with information.[1]

III

The commons' granting of money meets the eye more than any of their other activities; it is therefore regarded, by the prevailing opinion, as "unmistakably the principal cause of their being summoned during the first generation".[2]

[1] The writs of election inform us further that other duties also were imposed on the representatives, and, indeed, that parliaments were summoned for that reason alone. Thus in 1300 and in 1313 the purpose of the summons was said to be "ad perambulationem in forestis faciendam" (*P.W.* I, 98, 30; II, ii, 164, 4), i.e. to make a land survey. The like is to be found at other times. I have only been concerned to discover the obligations on the members which, because they were customary and obvious, were not at all mentioned; for these must have been most of all before the mind of Edward I in connexion with his new creation.

[A careful comparison of the lists of collectors of subsidy and of those elected to attend the parliaments raises doubts as to the correctness of Riess's view. The largest number of commons appointed to collect a subsidy was twenty-three, in 1295, the next highest numbers of the reigns of Edward I and Edward II being twenty-one in 1297 and 1309, and fifteen in 1316. During the following reign the number tended to diminish, the highest being twelve in 1372.

Such figures do not seem sufficient to justify the belief that a principal motive for summoning parliaments was to make the elected members personally responsible for the collection of the aids they had granted.

To understand the commons' repeated petitions that none of themselves should be appointed a collector of the subsidy they had granted, it should be observed that sheriffs, escheators, and even justices of the peace appear to have been exempt from this service. This I infer from the fact that certain men who were named in commissions for the collection of parliamentary subsidies were discharged on its being shown that they already held one of these local offices (e.g. *Cal. Fine Rolls*, VI, 273; VIII, 198). Doubtless the knights and burgesses who had attended a parliament regarded their right to consideration as equally strong and there would, of course, be no men to whom the collection of an aid could be more distasteful than those who had concurred in the grant. It is not surprising, therefore, that they should seek to free themselves from this liability.

But the class from which the collectors were drawn was comparatively small, and the number of men who could at any time be chosen would be reduced, not only by the exemption of the holders of the various local offices, but by the military service in which many men of this class were engaged. Thus it is natural that the central government should have resisted the commons' demand which would have further limited its choice and, when it became necessary to grant the petition, should have endeavoured at least to secure the assistance of the knights and burgesses in finding suitable collectors.]

[2] Gneist, *Englische Verfassungsgeschichte*, p. 361. In the English literature this view is most strongly represented by Hallam: "To grant money was, therefore, the main object of their meeting..." (*Constitutional History of England*, Chandos Classics edition, p. 24).

In the foregoing investigations two other "principal objects" have already been pointed out; the question is whether the granting of taxes was of equally outstanding importance, whether the new institution was in reality brought into existence for this purpose also.

In the first place, we have here also to distinguish, more sharply than the English scholars have done, the differences between our modern institutions and those with which we are concerned in the Middle Ages. In the modern state, the taxes with which the cost of administration is met are permanently established by law. On the other hand, the assent of parliament to the payments that are to be made is required annually; for the annual budget is produced in the form of a law to be in force for one year. But in the Middle Ages only the granting of the revenue was concerned; the taxes, assented to only for once, had always to be again granted, "subsidies to be voted".

Gneist, of course, fully realized this distinction, and therefore compares the position of the English system of taxation in the thirteenth century only with that of the Continent during the Middle Ages, to which it is, in form, very similar. Nevertheless, it is just here that a distinction between English and German constitutional life, resulting from a difference in historical development and general conceptions, is manifest.

In Germany the opinion prevailed that the central government had to pay for the administration of the country out of the income of the royal domain and the profits of the "Regalia"; only from good will, only as a special concession, did the estates help their lord to bear the heavy burdens which his duties as a ruler imposed upon him.

On the other hand, it was a lasting effect of the Norman Conquest that the king, as overlord, to a great extent imposed taxes and subsidies on his subjects. So arbitrarily was this power used, and so harshly were the orders of the royal exchequer carried out by the sheriffs, that the barons, capable as they were of armed resistance, rose as one man against the monarchy, and, in a vigorous struggle that filled the whole of the thirteenth century, endeavoured, above all, to win security from arbitrary and unendurable taxation.[1] After victory had been won by the

---

[1] No fewer than twenty-six of the sixty-two articles of Magna Carta concern this subject.

sword, they made their peace with the king on this basis: they recognized their liability to taxation, but made the amount to be raised on each occasion dependent on an express understanding between the king and all his tenants-in-chief. Only in this way did they hope to be taxed moderately and uniformly.

But the articles of Magna Carta that refer to the granting of taxes were soon entirely omitted from the confirmations;[1] at favourable moments the king always reverted to the former unrestricted liability. The victorious and popular Edward I lived in the consciousness of his unlimited right all the more because as heir to the throne he had taken up arms in its defence.[2] Consequently, in the midst of the war, the united barons, in 1297, again came forward with their old demand. By joining with the newly instituted lower house they believed that they could enforce the provisions that had been struck out of Magna Carta only because these had seemed incapable of practical fulfilment. In the traditional legal language, Latin, they drew up their plan: "No tallage or aid shall for the future be imposed by us or our heirs in our kingdom without the will and common assent of the archbishops and bishops, and other prelates; of the earls, barons, knights and burgesses, and of the other free men of our kingdom."[3] As we know, long negotiations took place the result of which was the following statute which the king issued in the language of ordinary intercourse, French: "and so we have conceded to the bishops and earls and barons and the whole community of the land, that for no necessity will we raise such contributions, or imposts, or levies from our kingdom, except with the common consent of the whole kingdom, saving the ancient contributions and levies that are due and accustomed".[4] The barons, it must be said, taking a broad view, had not limited their demand to their own class but had extended it to the representatives of the counties and towns. But the precise expressions of their draft— "knights", "burgesses"—are rendered colourless in the statute;

---

[1] 1217, 1224 and always after that year, see Gneist, *Englische Verfassungsgeschichte*, p. 259, n.

[2] He repeatedly seized the wool of the merchants and the treasures of the Church. In 1294 he demanded from the clergy half of their income.

[3] Also printed by Gneist, *Englische Verfassungsgeschichte*, p. 366, n.

[4] Likewise printed by Gneist, *loc. cit.*

only "the whole community of the land" stands beside the "bishops, earls, barons".[1] This already points to what is essential in the compromise. But still more decisive is the clause: "saving the ancient contributions and levies that are due and accustomed".

Here two classes of taxes are clearly distinguished: ancient taxes, and those of more recent date. Now, from time immemorial no new taxes had been invented; but about eighty years earlier a part of the taxes had assumed another character. Without having been established by law, the right of the barons to consent to the imposition of taxes was, in practice, under Henry III, "secured by more than twenty cases of precedent, and that as well by refusals as by grants".[2] The counties and towns, however, were always taxed without their consent.

Edward I, then, answered the question put to him thus, that he was not granting a new right, but that he would cease to regard the events of his father's reign as revolutionary; he recognized the cases of precedent, and therewith the right of the bishops and barons to grant taxes; to the merely actual concessions of his father he gave the sanction of law. It was just this legal and inviolable assurance that was of consequence to the ecclesiastics and barons; they brought it about that the new statute incorporated in the fundamental law of the country, Magna Carta, should be thrice confirmed along with this (1299, 1300, 1301). Thus, the right of assenting to taxation was never again called in question as far as it concerned the barons. But from the towns and counties, to which, indeed, nothing had been conceded, Edward himself, after this time, raised taxes concerning which he had not consulted them.

The king naturally believed that he would be giving away none of his rights if he allowed the assembled representatives of the counties and boroughs likewise to assent to the amount of taxes which he deemed necessary, and which, in any case, he intended to impose. Thus, indeed, he escaped in a convenient

---

[1] The "tote la communaute" seems to me quite as noncommittal as the "alii praelati", the "alii liberi homines" in the draft. In the contest with Henry III the community of tenants-in-chief had always described themselves as "communitas terrae" (Gneist, *Englische Verfassungsgeschichte*, p. 270). And this vague expression has no more definite meaning here.

[2] Gneist, *Englische Verfassungsgeschichte*, p. 267.

way the odium of making an oppressive imposition. But for a long time to come both parties remained aware of their legal position; the commons did not venture to refuse taxes, and only in a very few exceptional cases, which can be explained by particular circumstances, did they dare to attach modest conditions to their grants.[1]

With regard to the significance of the statute of 1297,[2] then, we are in opposition to the prevailing opinion. We deny that the right of granting taxes was thereby conceded to the counties and towns, and emphasize the point that it was mentioned only in the draft, not in the statute itself. The prevailing opinion is based on the fact that in a judicial decision of 1638, the force of law was accorded also to this draft. But a judicial pronouncement of nearly 350 years later can prove little with regard to the true position in 1297; and it must entirely give way before a contrary interpretation of contemporaries who were directly concerned. And what can be more indicative of the true opinion of contemporaries than legal agreements, which most certainly proceed from a keen understanding of the state of affairs, and a careful consideration of all the factors?

Therefore a contract of Edward II with the city of London, concerning a loan, can best inform us as to how people in the first generation of parliament regarded the commons' right of granting taxes. The king accepted forty pounds as payment in advance for the next subsidy; he gave a receipt for this, and instead of interest gave an equivalent concession. The citizens were promised that "we will in no wise cause any tax to be imposed or collected, individually or in common, from them, their goods and chattels, their lands, tenements, or rents, in the aforesaid city or its suburb, before our next parliament".[3] If under so weak a king as Edward II London, the only electoral district for which the Great Charter of 1215 had demanded the right of granting taxes, in spite of the obvious embarrassment of the

---

[1] Moreover, they submitted to taxes which they had not granted.
[2] "De tallagio non concedendo."
[3] "Quod tallagium aliquod separatim per capita vel in communi supra ipsos, bona et catalla terras et tenementa aut redditus suos in Civitate praedicta vel suburbio eiusdem ante proximum parliamentum nostrum assideri vel de eisdem levari nullatenus faciemus" (*P.W.* II, ii, Appendix 85, 38 (16 December 1314)).

king, regarded it as a privilege to be freed from arbitrary taxation even until the next parliament, there is in this the strongest imaginable acknowledgement that, as yet, no right of granting taxes had been conceded to the counties and boroughs.[1]

In 22 Edward III the commons granted three times the whole ordinary subsidy; at the same time they imposed on the impecunious king the condition that "in future no tallage or forced loan or other tax should be imposed by the king's council without the grant and assent of the commons in parliament, and that this should be expressed in a statute".[2] If the fundamental law of the land existing since the time of Edward I had really contained what historians have generally seen therein, why was the demand for a new statute necessary? Why did not the commons at least refer to this law?[3]

Herewith the supposition of there being a recognized right of the commons to grant taxes is, in my opinion, entirely destroyed; there was no compelling necessity for the king to summon the lower house when he required money.

But the moral advantages of a tax which had been granted, even if only formally granted, over one that was arbitrarily raised are not to be under-estimated. We assert only this: beside the two principal purposes mentioned above, this ethical consideration can have no real importance. Since it did not regularly come into force, but was equally often kept in the background, it lacked the value of principle which is so essential for moral power. Since, on the other hand, the subjects never had the possibility of insuring themselves by voluntary high taxation even against further unlimited arbitrary impositions, it loses all practical importance.[4]

[1] [This agreement is also an indication of the difficulty of levying tallage. See M. V. Clarke, *Medieval Representation and Consent*, pp. 272–3.]
[2] Gneist, *Englische Verfassungsgeschichte*, p. 369, n. 2b.
[3] The commons renewed their petition in 11 Richard II and the king gave the answer: "Le Roi le voet, sauvant son auncien droit" (*Rot. Parl.* III, 247, 31). After this concession the Commons' right to grant taxes was respected to the time of the Tudors. [Riess has overlooked the two statutes made in the parliament of April 1340 which, in return for the exceptionally heavy taxation voted at that time, laid it down that henceforth customs and aids were not to be levied without the consent of the magnates and Commons, and that in parliament (*Statutes of the Realm*, I, 289, 290).]
[4] The immense expenses of the representation of the country are also to be considered. Stubbs has estimated that the representatives of 1405 re-

CONCLUSION

The lower house was really created in order to make possible
the control of the provincial administration and in order that,
for important public business of a financial character, responsible
and trustworthy persons might be enlisted.

On the other hand, the right of assenting to the levying of
taxes is, in the first generation, merely of a formal nature; it
attained greater importance only gradually, through the force
of custom and favourable circumstances.

ceived not less than £5000 for expenses, whereas only £6000 were granted
to the king (*Constitutional History*, III, 56). However, on account of the
shorter duration of parliaments, the disproportion had never previously been
so great. [The supreme importance which Maitland and other writers attributed to the judicial functions of early parliaments led to the adoption, with
regard to their taxing powers, of views similar to those of Riess, though
how far this was due to Riess's work is uncertain. Several recent writers,
however, have found cause for thinking that the interpretation of Stubbs
came nearer to the truth. See M. V. Clarke, *Mediaeval Representation and
Consent*, especially pp. 278–316; C. H. McIlwain, in *Cambridge Medieval
History*, VII, 678; Carl Stephenson, *Taxation and Representation in the
Middle Ages* (Haskins Anniversary Essays); J. G. Edwards, *The "Plena
Potestas" of English Parliamentary Representatives* (Oxford Essays presented
to H. E. Salter).]

CHAPTER II

GENERAL REGULATIONS *for* ELECTIONS
ELECTORAL DISTRICTS

BEFORE the time of the Lancastrians the method of holding elections in England had not been fixed by law; instead of this the prescriptions of Edward I which had become established by custom, and special regulations which were occasionally introduced, served as models and set the standard. We shall here draw attention to some generally accepted rules.

1. Just as the place and time of the parliament was entirely dependent on the will of the king (that parliament should be held at least annually was only an approximate assurance, which was hardly regarded as binding), so the time of the year for the election is also not laid down. That the meeting of the parliament would be appointed for a time that was not close at hand was obvious from the summons; for first the writs for holding the election had to be forwarded to the electing bodies, and then time allowed for the election of representatives and for their journey to the place of meeting. Corresponding to these conditions, an intervening period of at least forty days was established as the minimum;[1] but for three exceptions[2] Edward I kept to this limit; usually he chose a still more distant time.[3] This remained the rule under his successors.

2. The writs of summons were issued to the sheriffs of the counties as the commissioners for the election, who were made responsible for the satisfactory and prompt discharge of the business. They had also to see to it that all the representatives had the requisite full power from their constituencies.[4]

---

[1] *Modus tenendi Parliamentum*, ed. Hardy, p. 3: "Summonitio parliamenti praecedere debet primum diem Parliamenti per quadraginta dies." This indeed goes back to Article 61 of Magna Carta.

[2] 14 June to 15 July 1290 = 31 days; 8 October to 12 November 1294 = 35 days; 15 September to 6 October 1297 = 21 days.

[3] 26 September 1300 to 20 January 1301 = 116 days; 12 November 1304 to 16 February 1305 = 96 days, and so forth.

[4] Thus it is said expressly in all the writs of summons "habeant plenam potestatem...".

Of the towns, London alone originally received a separate writ;[1] only from the time of Edward III were a number of other important towns very gradually added.[2]

3. The duration of the mandate was not fixed, but it had force only for the coming session, however long or short that might be. Consequently new elections had to be held every time a parliament was summoned. The king, it is true, occasionally re-summoned those who had been elected to the previous parliament; but in all these cases the new parliament appears to have been only a continuation of the old after an interruption caused by particular circumstances.[3]

But of the utmost importance is the formation of the electoral districts. In the first place thirty-seven counties which had existed since Anglo-Saxon times, and which constituted self-contained administrative bodies almost of the modern type, each formed an electoral district regularly returning two representatives. It was here a matter of indifference, whether this district contained seven square miles as did Rutland, or 132 as did Lincoln; whether two counties were united under the direction of a single sheriff (as was usually the case with Oxford and Berks, Nottingham and Derby, Somerset and Dorset, Bedford and Buckingham, Leicester and Warwick, Norfolk and Suffolk, Surrey and Sussex) or whether they were administered separately.

Then to these must be added the towns which were characterized by their exemption from the hundred court, and the formation of their own inferior courts of justice, courts leet.[4]

---

[1] The first example comes from 24 June 1283 (R.D.P. I, Appendix p. 50).

[2]
Bristol.	From 50 Edward III.	R.D.P. II, 671.	
York.	,, 20 Richard II.	,,	757.
Newcastle.	,, 3 Henry IV.	,,	783.
Norwich.	,, 5 Henry IV.	,,	792.
Lincoln.	,, 14 Henry IV.	,,	815.
Kingston upon Hull.	,, 23 Henry VI.	,,	909.
Southampton⎱ Nottingham⎰	,, 28 Henry VI.	,,	925.
Coventry.	,, 38 Henry VI.	,,	943.
Canterbury.	,, 2 Edward IV.	,,	959.

[3] For example, on 26 September 1300 (P.W. I, 90); 11 October 1311 (P.W. II, ii, 58); etc.

[4] Merewether and Stephens, *History of Boroughs*, I, 114, 131. [Here, Riess has misused the term *Court Leet* which was, of course, a franchise court

They, too, according to the wording of the summons should each be represented by two members; since in all the writs for the elections it is said: the sheriffs of the counties "shall cause to be elected two citizens from every city and two burgesses from every borough". But because these directions were never carried out in practice, and always only a fraction of the English towns were summoned and represented, this point has already been for a long time a matter of controversy.[1]

I believe that we can come nearer to a solution of the unsettled problems with regard to the summoning of the boroughs only if we first examine the extant returns, which the sheriffs sent into chancery, more carefully than has so far been done. This I have endeavoured to do, at least for the reigns of Edward I and Edward II, for which alone the returns are printed.

A. *Concerning the designation of the towns in the election returns*

The sheriffs sent the writ for the election, which they had received, or a copy of it, to the bailiffs of every town in which an election was to be held;[2] this is shown by numerous explicit remarks in the election returns.[3] On the back of the writ which he had received, the sheriff wrote not only the report of the election but, very often also, abbreviations, most of which can be recognized as designations of towns.[4]

which might be burghal or seignorial, for enforcing the frankpledge system, for the presentment of offences and the punishment of minor offences (Pollock and Maitland, *History of English Law*, I, 531–2). Far higher powers were exercised by the borough courts and these were not always inferior to the county court except when the royal justices were present in the latter.]

[1] Stubbs (*Constitutional History*, II, 232 ff., also n. 1) refuses any deeper research with the words: "yet the matter is not so clear but that...expressions are found that might lead to a different conclusion".

[2] This will be discussed more fully below.

[3] "Pro civibus civitatis Cantuariae retornatum fuit istud breve ballivis libertatis ejusdem civitatis", *P.W.* I, 96, 23. The same is said, *P.W.* I, 143, 18, for Essex and Hertford; *P.W.* I, 151, 38, for Somerset and Dorset; *P.W.* II, ii, 48, 12, for Lincoln; *P.W.* II, ii, 51, 17, for Oxford and Berkshire; *P.W.* II, ii, 143, 55, for Gloucester.

[4] E.g. *P.W.* I, 126, 49 (20 July to 29 September 1302):
  Somerset' and Dorset'.
    In dorso.
retr. Brug.
  Baa.
  Taunton.
  Ivelchester.

Then followed the regular election return with the names of the knights of the shire and burgesses.[1] These abbreviated notes on the dorse are, I believe, cursory memoranda which the sheriff made for his own use, to remind himself to which towns he had forwarded the royal letter with the order to hold an election.[2]

We have then, in very many instances, traces of the sending of the writs, that is, of the actual summons of the boroughs. At the same time, we have also the places to which the command to hold an election was directed, and these too will prove very instructive.

or for the same counties, *P.W.* I, 126, 50 (13 September to 14 October 1302):

	Somerset'.	Dorset'
	Taunton.	Ré p. pro Warham et Sheftebu.
	Brug.	
	Well.	
	Baa.	
	Ivelchester.	
A.p.e.	Wachet.	

also for Norfolk and Suffolk, *P.W.* II, ii, 49, 13:

P.est.	Norwyc.	P.e.	Gern.
	St Edm.		Don.
	Gipp.		Orford.
	Ffreth.		

[1] So, regularly, for Norfolk and Suffolk, *P.W.* II, ii, 8, 30, 49, 62, 86, 108, 145, 189, 205, 225, 240, 253, 304. But also for Kent, *P.W.* I, 144; Southampton, *P.W.* I, 175, II, ii, 12, 29; Wiltshire, *P.W.* II, ii, 35, 115; and so forth.

[2] This view can be proved by the following evidence: 1. The report often states such and such towns are sending representatives; such and such have not answered. Usually the names of both classes together correspond exactly to the abbreviations above, e.g. *P.W.* II, ii, 12, 29, Southampton, 1307: In dorso. Sutht. Portesm̃. Wyntoñ. Anđ Ins̃. Epc̃. In panello. Representatives for: Wyntonie, Portsmouth, Andevere: "...returnatum fuit Ballivis libertatum Ville Sutht., [Insula Vecta], et Episcopi Wintonie, qui nullum inde mihi dederunt responsum". Likewise *P.W.* I, 175, 42, where nine abbreviations are given; the representatives of seven are named and one town designated as negligent. Further, *P.W.* II, ii, 115, the return for Wiltshire, and so forth. The accompanying abbreviations are an argument for my view: (*a*) "retr." is obviously "returnatum". (*b*) "p.e." means "perlatum est", for the abbreviation mark over "p." is that used elsewhere when "er" is omitted and passages like "p.e. omnibus Ballivis in co" (*P.W.* II, ii, 13, 22, Wiltshire), "p.e. cibus Bur...in crast (*P.W.* II, ii, 186, 10, Cornwall) admit of no other interpretation. (*c*) "Ro. R. ht. Cantuar. ht." (*P.W.* I, i, 144) is to be interpreted "Roffensis Returnum habet, Cantuaria habet"; similarly *P.W.* II, ii, 270, 37. (*d*) "ta Weng, ta Newport" (*P.W.* II, ii, 202, Essex) clearly means "tradita".

B. *The average number of boroughs represented*

To begin with, we may now proceed to determine the average number of towns that were summoned and represented under Edward I and Edward II somewhat more precisely than has been done by Stubbs[1] and Gneist.[2]

In the "Contents" of Palgrave's *Parliamentary Writs*, I, 203 names are registered as those mentioned in the returns, and by simply subtracting 37—the number of the counties—the number 166 is reached.[3] But even if one takes exception to this high number and, with Prynne, places the number of real parliamentary boroughs at 107, the false impression is still created that these at least were regularly summoned and represented. In reality, in the eight parliaments of Edward I for which we have adequate returns, 604 deputations from towns were present,[4] thus, on the average, 75. Besides, about 60 summonses which had no effect are to be found in the text of the returns and in the abbreviations on the dorse;[5] we thus arrive at the number of 664 summonses, or an average of 83.

It agrees well with this that in the important parliament of January 1307, according to the extant certification (*P.W.* I, ii,

[1] *Constitutional History*, II, 235; III, 448.

[2] *Kommunalverfassung*, I, 200; *Englische Verfassungsgeschichte*, p. 388.

[3] Probably Gneist counts London with the counties and so comes to 165 boroughs.

[4] [Riess, like his contemporaries, made the mistake of assuming that all who were returned to parliament actually attended. Thus, here and elsewhere he uses the phrase "were present" when it would have been more accurate to say "were returned". Professor Pollard (*Evolution of Parliament*, pp. 116, 316–19) was the first to point out the unreliability of the *Sheriffs Returns* as proofs of parliamentary service. He maintained that the writs *de expensis* were as a rule the only trustworthy evidence of attendance, and from a comparison of the numbers obtained from these records with those yielded by the *Sheriffs' Returns*, he concluded that many men, especially among the burgesses, who were elected failed to go to parliament. More recent research, however, especially that by Miss May McKisack, who in many borough records has found evidence of the payment of representatives whose names do not occur in the enrolled writs *de expensis*, has modified this view (*The Parliamentary Representation of the English Boroughs during the Middle Ages*, Oxford, 1932. See also J. G. Edwards, *The Personnel of the Commons in Parliament under Edward I and Edward II*, Essays presented to Thomas Frederick Tout, Manchester, 1925; and K. L. Wood-Legh, "The knights' attendance in the parliaments of Edward III", *E.H.R.* XLVII, 1932). Probably the number of those who actually served in parliament considerably exceeded that yielded by the writs *de expensis*, but was less than the number of those returned.]

[5] The Calendar takes no account of this.

187), 174 borough representatives[1] from 87 towns were present, for the summonses to this parliament were exceptionally numerous.

All these figures become interesting only by comparison with those of the following reign; the question is whether the leading authorities are right in assuming a gradual increase in the numbers.[2]

Now in eighteen parliaments under Edward II there were altogether 1083 representations, thus an average of 60. Again with the help of the abbreviations, 1209 summonses can be traced, or an average number of about 67. Here also the average number is in agreement with the list drawn up in the chancery (*P.W.* ii, ii, 311), where 128 Citizens and Burgesses are enumerated.[3] It is apparent, therefore, that the average number of boroughs that were represented diminished in the course of the first generation from 75 to 60. But what is far more significant is the fact that, although more than a quarter of the towns that were summoned under Edward I very soon disappear from the list of those summoned because they appointed no representatives, the proportion of representations to summonses under Edward II is quite as unfavourable as under his predecessor. Under Edward I the eight times 83 summonses are divided among 166 towns, each of which was summoned at least once, and so could have claimed, by this precedent, to be regularly summoned. Thus the number of towns admitted to representation bears to the average number that were represented the proportion of 166 to 75, or 42 to 19. Since under Edward II the number of towns that were summoned declines to 123, and that of those represented to an average of 60, the proportion of 41 to 20, which is not materially different, is yielded.

From these figures we observe that the numbers of summonses

[1] When Gneist (*Kommunalverfassung*, I, 201) gives 200 borough representatives, the thirty-one, who at the end of the certificate are recommended for remuneration to their mayors and bailiffs, are included. But these are already named in the certificate itself. The error, however, goes back to Hallam, *Constitutional History*, Chandos Classics edition, p. 77.

[2] Gneist, *Englische Verfassungsgeschichte*, p. 388.

[3] To these must be added however the representatives of Launceston, Bodmin and Helstone, who were overlooked, but of whom we have information in the extant return.

and of representations diminished equally and that the "honour of representation" was in nowise more sought after under Edward II than under his predecessor.

Since in these abbreviations on the dorse we have found traces of the former procedure of the summons, and have, by the examination of the numbers, obtained some information as to the course of development, we can now scrutinize more closely the real problem of the borough representation and ask the questions: According to what principles were the towns, that should be summoned, chosen? By what signs are they distinguished from the multitude of others that were never, or only temporarily, summoned?

Here we cannot sufficiently emphasize the fundamental difference between the general modern conception of the value and importance of the right of representation and the conception held in the Middle Ages. When the English towns, in obedience to the king's command, sent their two representatives to parliament, this obviously appeared to them a burdensome duty; they endeavoured as far as possible to free themselves from this burden, which imposed on the community a financial sacrifice, and on its representatives wearisome labour.[1]

This is proved not only by the numerous cases in which the sheriff states expressly that he had sent the royal mandate to certain towns but had received no answer,[2] but also by countless instances in which, according to the abbreviations on the dorse, a summons must have been issued, but in which no notice is taken of this in the returns.[3]

Moreover, exemptions from this duty are not wanting. Thus

---

[1] Stubbs (*Constitutional History*, III, 616) mentions this essential difference only quite casually. It receives somewhat more attention from Cox, *Antient Parliamentary Elections*, p. 157.

[2] *P.W.* I, 95, 2, Hertford: "Pro burgensibus villate de Scto Albano returnum istius brevis factum fuit balivo libertatis Scti Albani. Qui nihil inde mihi responderunt." Other examples are: *P.W.* I, 123, 37, Villa Scti Edmundi; *P.W.* I, 150, 33, Wyndesore; *P.W.* I, 151, 38, Civitas Bathon; *P.W.* II, ii, 44, 1, Donestaple; *P.W.* II, ii, 46, 6 Skardeburgh; *P.W.* II, ii, 97, 11, Gippewyci; *P.W.* II, ii, 253, 63, Donewyci; *P.W.* II, ii, 358, 32, Bristol; etc.; in short, large and small towns in all the counties.

[3] E.g. Villa Scti Edmundi, Villa de Lenn, Villa Orford, *P.W.* II, ii, 49; Mitford, *P.W.* II, ii, 108; Warham, *P.W.* II, ii, 10, 11; Dounton, *P.W.* II, ii, 35, 40; 228, 30; 242; etc.

in 6 Richard II it was granted that Colchester, on account of the expenses of building new town walls, need send no representatives to parliament for five years (*Rot. Parl.* III, 395, 19), Torrington in Devon was even exempted for ever from parliamentary representation. In the document of Edward III dealing with this it is said: "for the inhabitants of Chepyngtoriton, who out of malice have been compelled to accept the burden of sending representatives to parliament (malitiose ad mittendum Homines ad Parliamenta, oneratis...). As it is shown that only since 24 Edward III has the sheriff out of malice included you in his report to our chancery as sending representatives, and we find no earlier example in our rolls, we exempt you from this heavy burden."[1]

We have, then, to do with a duty which, in the ordinary course, extended equally to all towns without distinction; accordingly the writs regularly require the sheriff to summon two representatives from every town. But it was not laid down what punishment should be inflicted if a town that had been summoned neglected its duty and sent no representatives. Indeed, in spite of the very numerous instances in which the chancery received information of such omissions, there is not a single example of the imposition of a punishment on the negligent community such as can be proved was inflicted on barons who were summoned and failed to appear.[2]

Only in a single instance is there a trace even of an excuse for non-attendance[3] such as regularly came to hand in the case of spiritual and lay peers who were absent.[4] In this respect there is a striking difference between the borough constituencies and the shires, which were represented most regularly, and on the

---

[1] Rymer, *Foedera*, H. III, pars II, p. 146. The statements are incorrect. For the rolls which the king had ostensibly caused to be searched prove that Torrington was represented in 1295, 1302 and at other times under Edward I and Edward II (*P.W.* I, 35, 11; 36, 12; 119, 23; etc.). [The citation from Rymer is inexact; the quotation proper begins at "as it is shown", what precedes this being only the Editor's heading.]

[2] Rymer, *Foedera*, H. II, pars III, p. 141. "...Mauritius filius Nicolai nuper amerciatus fuit in centum Marcis, eo quod non venit ad parliamentum." [This evidence is irrelevant, as it refers to the Irish, not to the English parliament. There is no evidence that barons were fined for failure to attend the latter. See M. V. Clarke, *Medieval Representation and Consent*, pp. 118, n. 2, 219–20.]

[3] *P.W.* II, ii, 145, 66.

[4] E.g. *P.W.* II, ii, 247, 45; 264; etc.

very few occasions of their non-attendance brought forward weighty reasons to excuse their absence.[1]

The chancery was not at all concerned with which boroughs were summoned, and which passed over, on any occasion; it allowed the sheriff to act entirely at his own discretion. Indeed, the sheriff of Bedfordshire and Buckinghamshire coolly stated in his return, on 6 October 1320, that with the exception of Bedford, which is sending representatives, "Non sunt plures Burgi in balliva mea" (*P.W.* II, ii, 221), whereas, in the *Nomina Villarum* of 1316, five other boroughs in Buckinghamshire are named[2] which in the reign of Edward I had sent members to parliament. But what is still more striking, as recently as 20 March 1319, Philip de Aylesbury, the predecessor of this sheriff, had at least summoned Wycombe,[3] which he again included, in 1322, when he was once more sheriff.[4] This case is only one among many[5] which all prove that the chancery (which received the returns, copied abstracts of them on to its rolls and caused them to be read aloud to prove the attendance in parliament) did not take the sheriff's business of summoning under its control.

In this absence of any rule imposed from above, we must of course refrain from seeking to lay down the principles under-

[1] *P.W.* I, 44, 21, Westmorland; *P.W.* I, 60, 36, Surrey and Sussex; *P.W.* I, 176, 44, Westmorland; *P.W.* II, ii, 145, 66, Northumberland. [Riess's comparison between the attendance of the knights and burgesses is, on the whole, just, but his remarks are not free from exaggeration. The excuses for the non-attendance of knights, which the sheriffs occasionally sent in to chancery, probably indicate only that these sheriffs were exceptionally painstaking, and can by no means be regarded as furnishing an exhaustive list of the instances in which knights of the shire failed to attend. This error might have been avoided by somewhat closer attention to the list of those present in the parliament of 1307, quoted elsewhere.]

[2] *P.W.* II, iii, 372-3: Amersham, Wendover, Aylesbury are mentioned; the names of the two boroughs in the hundred of Desborough which, according to Palgrave's note, are illegible, are Wycombe and Marlow, as is shown by the election returns.

[3] It had been summoned regularly until then.

[4] *P.W.* II, ii, 248.

[5] Some particularly clear examples may be cited here: besides York and Scarborough, "non sunt plures Civitates nec Burgi in Com. Eborum" is in *P.W.* II, ii, 337, but in the immediately preceding and ensuing parliaments Kingston [Hull] was also represented (*P.W.* II, ii, 301, 357). Except Colchester, states the sheriff of Essex and Hertfordshire, "non sunt plures Civitates seu Burgi in Balliva mea" (*P.W.* II, ii, 357-8). But according to p. 301 Hertford, pp. 269, 250 Hertford and Stortford, p. 223 Hertford, Stortford and Berkhamsted were summoned.

lying the arrangements which imposed the duty of election on a number of towns and freed others from representation. For during our whole period directions on this point are wanting. Even when Richard II attempted, at least to some extent, to settle and permanently to regularize the fluctuating summonses which were influenced by all manner of arbitrary acts, he found no other rule than the traditional and customary usage; his idea could only be to prevent a further decline.[1]

We must, however, enquire into the causes which without restricting the summons to a particular class of town led to a gradual diminution in the number of those that were summoned. The answer which Stubbs[2] and Gneist, following him,[3] give cannot, in my opinion, suffice. According to these scholars:

1. The counties which were prominent on account of sea-borne commerce and industry, Devon, Dorset, Kent,[4] Wiltshire and Sussex, were especially considered in the summoning of the boroughs.

But to this argument, which even in favourable circumstances could only be subsidiary, we can by no means assent. For how can it be applied to Wiltshire, which is entirely cut off from the sea coast? But, above all, it is well known that precisely in the fourteenth century the population of England was almost exclusively occupied with agriculture and the production of wool, and left the commerce and industries to German, Lombard and Flemish strangers. And for trade with these, the towns at the mouths of rivers, especially Bristol, King's Lynn, Norwich, Lincoln, Newcastle, Great Yarmouth and Ipswich, were far more important than the coastal towns on the stormy Channel.[5]

---

[1] *Rot. Parl.* iii, 124, 16 (5 Richard II): "...Et si ascun Viscount du Roialme soit desore negligent en faisant les Retournes des Briefs du Parlement, ou q'il face entrelesser hors des ditz Retornes aucunes Citees ou Burghs queux sont tenuz & d'auncien temps soloient venir au Parlement, soit puniz en manere q'estoit acustumez d'estre fait en le cas d'aunciente."

[2] *Constitutional History*, iii, 449.

[3] *Englische Verfassungsgeschichte*, p. 389.

[4] Only two towns in Kent are summoned, whereas there were six other counties with two boroughs, four with three, one with four, and one with as many as six that were likewise summoned which do not fall into Stubbs's favoured class. See *Constitutional History*, iii, 448, n. 4 and 449, nn. 1, 2.

[5] In the list of Staple towns which Gneist publishes (*Kommunalver-fassung*, i, 111) only one town of these counties appears: Exeter in Devon. [Actually the list also includes Canterbury and Chichester.] Likewise, of all the twenty-one towns which, on account of their great importance, were

2. Again, the second cause, according to these scholars, the greater or lesser distance from London, cannot be seriously alleged. Since the very counties that were nearest to London, Bedfordshire, Buckinghamshire, Northamptonshire, Oxfordshire had each only one parliamentary borough, while the little county of Cornwall, in spite of the fact that, except for Northumberland, it is the farthest from London, is among those with the most parliamentary boroughs, namely six.

3. But I wish especially to oppose Stubbs's "most important cause".[1] Without the slightest documentary evidence, Stubbs assumes that the boroughs which had not been summoned were only required to contribute at the rate for the county, one-fifteenth, because they had not participated in the higher grant made by the Citizens and Burgesses.[2] Not without reason, however, do all the writs for the collection of taxes contain some such generalizing expression as "the taxes which the citizens and burgesses and the commons of all the cities and boroughs of the kingdom have granted".[3] Moreover, definite confirmation of our view, opposed to that of Stubbs, may be adduced. In the year 1319 a twelfth was granted by the towns; the command to collect this proportion was sent also to Coventry, although it had not been summoned;[4] to Grantham, which was never summoned till the time of Edward IV; to Portsmouth, which was at least not represented,[5] and to others.

Thus, then, these possibilities which previous research has put forward with no actual support must be entirely set aside.[6]

summoned by the exchequer in 1283, Exeter again is the only one from all these counties.

[1] So also Gneist, *Englische Verfassungsgeschichte*, p. 389.

[2] [For a detailed discussion of this subject see J. F. Willard, *Taxation boroughs and Parliamentary boroughs*, in Historical Essays in honour of James Tait, Manchester, 1933.]

[3] *P.W.* II, ii, 116: "quae cives et burgenses communitatesque omnium Civitatum et Burgorum ejusdem regni concesserunt".

[4] *P.W.* II, ii, 209, 74.   [5] *P.W.* II, ii, 209, 72.

[6] The fundamental error is that Stubbs always has in mind an ordering by the central government, which in fact did not exist. In his *Select Charters*, Stubbs tries also to point out the legal basis for such ordering: "...it was in the power of the crown or its advisers to increase or diminish the number of boroughs represented—a power based on the doctrine that their privilege was the gift of the crown and their status, historically, that of royal demesne" (*Select Charters* IV, ed. 1881, p. 44). As if even a trace of this doctrine, which the scholars of the eighteenth century created, could be found in the Middle Ages.

An explanation of this diversity of practice may be found in the suggestion that the summoning of the boroughs was dependent upon the sheriff alone; this raises the following questions: Had the different towns to some extent different administrative arrangements? Does this result in important differences in the mode of transacting business between the sheriffs and the local administration of the towns? An investigation of these matters has, I believe, produced notable results. The fact that some towns had a magnate as their lord and were apparently inherited in his family, while others recognized the king himself in this position,[1] did not bring about an administrative difference; it is indeed only the formal right of confirming the bailiffs, and, perhaps some insignificant perquisites, which were treated as the possession of private jurisdiction.[2]

Of far greater significance is the exemption from the sheriff's power of direct interference in all occurrences within the town. I assume with Merewether and Stephens that it was essential

---

[1] The former opinion that only towns which had the king as their lord were to be summoned (still represented in *R.D.P.*) has been thoroughly disproved by Merewether and Stephens. Cox (*Antient Parliamentary Elections*, pp. 148–62) again has brought together from the *Rotuli Hundredorum* of the time of Henry III numerous examples of lords' towns that were summoned to parliament. [The two volumes published under this title contain returns to six inquests of the reigns of Henry III and Edward I. See H. M. Cam, *The Hundred and the Hundred Rolls*, p. 47.] The number can easily be much increased from the *Nomina Villarum* of 1316, which is printed in *P.W.* II, iii, 301 ff. and by an examination of the abbreviations on the dorse. For example, there must be added: Barnstaple, Plympton, Torrington, Totnes, Honiton, Sutton, Bradninch, Oakhampton, Tavistock in Devon [*P.W.* II, iii, 383 ff.].

[2] These rights arose, without doubt, from the circumstance that everywhere there was a lord, the owner of the woods and the common pasture which all those who belonged to the place had the right of using (*Servitutsrecht*). In England there was no question of a delegation of royal authority to great lords of the land. [Here Riess has under-estimated the difference between royal and seignorial boroughs. The king was almost invariably ready to sell to his burgesses the right to manage their own affairs; whilst other lords of towns, and particularly the monasteries, were often extremely tenacious of their ancient rights and did all in their power to prevent the boroughs on their domains from becoming self-governing. The contests between the townsmen and the monasteries of St Alban's and Bury St Edmund's are well known. One of the means by which the former sought to establish their independence was by sending representatives to parliament, which is probably the first occasion on which a borough desired to be represented.

During the past few years the position of monastic and other seignorial boroughs has been much studied. See especially J. Tait, *The Mediaeval English Borough*; N. M. Trenholme, *The English Monastic Boroughs* and M. D. Lobel, *The Borough of Bury St Edmund's*.]

for the full liberty of a district or a town to have the right of the
return of writs (*plenum returnum brevium*), that is, the privilege
that everything that was to be undertaken within the franchise,
even general measures concerning the county and the kingdom,
should be carried out only by the officials of the liberty themselves, who must be required to do this through the return of
writs. For only by thus building up a rigorously exclusive
subordinate district was it possible to keep the hated sheriff at
a distance.[1]

But through this institution two kinds of liberties, suited
to the administrative organization of the county, separated
themselves from the shire.[2]

Every county, that is to say, was divided into a number of
hundreds, thus, Hampshire into thirty-eight, Cambridgeshire
into fourteen, Huntingdonshire into four. These hundreds, in
their turn, contained a number of local groups, which are
commonly called vills. At the head of the hundreds stood bailiffs,
who counted as officials of their superior, the sheriff, and who
were at all times subject to his control and interference. The
local authorities[3] of the vills were in a similar position with
regard to the bailiff of their hundred, whether each one was
separate, or whether, as in Hampshire, two or three were united
to form one hamlet.

The immunities which broke through this official organization
were established in the following ways:

1. If a local group within the hundred so shut itself off that
all executive measures were carried out by its own officials (as
a rule on the information of the bailiff of the hundred, but
without his control or power of objecting), a borough was
created. The ordinary business between the central government
and the constable of such a borough went through the hands of
the sheriff and the bailiff of the hundred concerned.[4]

[1] Merewether and Stephens, *History of Boroughs*, I, 490, citing Statute of
Westminster, anno 1285, cap. 39; similarly, p. 494. How important and
coveted this right was is shown by examples such as I, 437, 447, 467, 478.
[2] In the following, I rely on the list of the hundreds, boroughs, vills, etc.,
which in 1316 was sent by the sheriffs into the chancery at the command of
Edward II. It is printed *P.W.* II, iii, 301 ff.
[3] At times the special title "Constable" is used for these.
[4] For example, a borough of this kind is Lynn, situated in the hundred of
Freebridge in Norfolk. On this account the returns for Lynn were sent from

2. If a borough or a city (the distinction between them is only one of name) was taken entirely out of the hundred and treated as an independent member of the county, it became a liberty which dealt directly with the sheriff; somewhat as our Prussian towns with more than ten thousand inhabitants are on a par with the "Kreise" and are subject only to the "Regierungs-präsident".

To the sheriff, of course, only such an exempt town appeared as a "liber Burgus", as is said in the *Nomina Villarum* with regard to Herefordshire: "Leominster, Burgus cum libertate (Dominus est Abbas de Radinge)", whereas Weobley borough is simply placed in its hundred. In Wiltshire it is said: "Civitas Nove Sarum (Dominus Epc. Sarum)...non est infra aliquod Hundredum."[1] Or, with regard to such a town, the sheriff observes that it has the *returnum brevium*, as is said of Exeter in the list for Devon: "Civitas Exonia in Comitatu Devon (Dominus ejusdem Rex) et habet returnum brevium."[2]

I believe that we can affirm this position for all the boroughs and cities which are enumerated along with the hundreds as districts of equal importance; with regard to the majority of them the returns fully confirm this.[3]

3. A peculiar position was occupied by those towns which lay within larger districts which were themselves liberties, and equal in rank to the hundreds.

In Devon, "Manerium de Uplym" is so specified, of which it is said "et habet returna similiter" (as Exeter); in Berkshire appear the "Libertas Abbatis de Bello de Brigetwaltone" and "Libertas Honoris Wallingford". Moreover, in Suffolk appear

the sheriff, in the first place to the bailiff of Freebridge (*P.W.* i, 123, 37). A summons to Lynn is indicated, therefore, by the abbreviation "Frech", on the dorse; thus: *P.W.* i, 97, 27, "Freth. p Lenn."; *P.W.* ii, ii, 49, 13, "ffreth."; also 62, 86, 108, 130, 145. The sheriff of Buckingham clearly alludes to these places which were subordinated to the bailiffs of the hundreds: "praedicta Hundreda,...infra quae sunt diversae libertates, quae habent returnum brevium" (*P.W.* ii, iii, 370).

[1] *P.W.* ii, iii, 346.
[2] Of many places, the election returns themselves contain the information that they enjoy this freedom. "Ballivi qui plenum returnum brevium habent" are mentioned, for example, for Worcester, *P.W.* ii, ii, 194, 32; 209, 76; Bedford, *P.W.* ii, ii, 200, 51; Hertford and Colchester, *P.W.* i, 143, 18; etc.
[3] Statements in the election returns confirm this almost regularly, thus: Civitas Cantuaria; Civitas Roffensis, *P.W.* ii, iii, 328, 14; 332, 60; Civitas Winton; Burgus de Portesmuthe; de Southampton, *P.W.* ii, iii, 345, 42, 43.

the liberties of St Etheldreda and St Edmunds, the first of which contained five and a half, the second as many as seven hundreds, whereas the district directly subject to the sheriff contained only seven and a half hundreds.[1] That commands were not issued direct to towns within liberties of this kind, but that the intermediation of the bailiffs of the liberty was necessary, is shown clearly by the sheriffs' returns; for example, to summon two burgesses from Windsor, the writ would be despatched to the chiefs of the liberty of the seven hundreds of Cookham and Bray, who had the right of transmitting all regulations and of carrying them out "qui habent returnum omnium brevium et executionem eorundem" (*P.W.* I, 150, 33, Oxon and Berks).

We see, then, that the towns within liberties were, on the whole, in the same position as those within hundreds, described in section I, except that the sheriff, when he wished, could deal directly with the latter, while in the case of the former he was bound to act through the bailiff of the liberty.[2]

4. Originally only London was on a par with the counties; it dealt directly with the chancery—as a return for Middlesex expresses it: "I report, that in the aforesaid county there is no city or borough except the city of London, which answers for itself as a corporation."[3]

To attain the same position was the object of a petition from Bristol: "...that the said town with its suburbs and surroundings may constitute an independent county".[4] Probably Bristol achieved its aim, and the natural consequence of this was that

[1] The difference between liberties and ordinary hundreds also comes out very clearly in the wording of the returns; e.g. *P.W.* I, 123, 37: "Et...feci praeceptum...Ballivo...de hundredo de Frechebrugge", whereas for the two liberties of Yarmouth and St Edmund's the expression "feci returnum" is used. The sheriff of Gloucester writes: "...retornatum fuit istud breve tam Ballivis libertatum de Hembury, Blidesle, Scti Briawell, Bysele, Fiscamp et Westm, qui habent returnum omnium brevium...et eciam Ballivis libertatum de Poukelchirche et Teukersbury, qui similiter habent returnum omnium brevium...", but "praeceptum fuit aliis Ballivis..." (*P.W.* I, 95).

[2] "Pro duobus Burgensibus de Burgo de Wynteneye [eligendis]...retornatum fuit Ballivo libertatis Dni Adomari de Valencia de Hundredo suo de Bampton pro eo quod Burgus de Wynteneye est infra libertatem praedictam..." (*P.W.* II, ii, 51, 17). This is indeed the clearest example.

[3] *P.W.* II, ii, 205, 65: "Et vobis significo quod non est aliqua Civitas seu Burgus in Comitatu praedicto praeterquam Civitas London, quae per se ipsam pro communitate respondet...."

[4] "...Que la dite Ville ovesque les Suburbes & Purceinte d'icelle soit Countee par soi" (*Rot. Parl.* II, 320, 31 (47 Edward III)).

soon thereafter, in 50 Edward III, it was summoned to parliament direct from the chancery.[1]

We now understand what a long and roundabout way some writs had to follow before they reached the borough authorities who had to execute them. Thus may be explained the fact that in the methods of summoning a remarkable diversity was developed. The sheriffs who were not too distant from London could easily retain the old customary way of transmitting writs; for the towns that were only taken out of the hundreds, they employed the usual services of the bailiffs of the hundreds.[2] In the case of more distant counties, this indirect way was a waste of time which might result in a serious delay of the answer affecting the parliament. In these circumstances most of the sheriffs adopted the expedient of sending the royal writ direct to the towns that were to be summoned. The sheriff of Devon, who, according to the abbreviation (P.W. II, ii, 5, 11), sent the command to Braunton in order to summon a borough within that hundred, later (P.W. II, ii, 249, 51) sent the summons direct to Barnstaple. Similarly, the sheriff of Wiltshire, as early as 1302, summoned Devizes direct—not the hundred of Roborough in which it lay;[3] further, in 1307, he summoned Bedwin—not as in 1302, the hundred of Kinwardstone; and in 1309, Ludgershall and Marlborough, direct, although both lay within hundreds. The same method of summoning was followed in Somerset and Dorset, where, for example, Shaftesbury and Melcombe were summoned direct and not through the bailiffs of the hundreds of Whiteway and Sixpenny.[4] In Cornwall, also, this method seems to have been in use, since in 1318 it is said: "p. e. omnibus Burg...in crast...".[5]

---

[1] Concerning the other towns that were summoned direct by the chancery there is nothing further in the printed material.

[2] For that reason the abbreviation on the dorse under Norfolk, "ffrech", for the hundred of Freebridge, in which Lynn, which was to be summoned, lay, always recurs, e.g. P.W. II, ii, 145, 64: "p.e. ffrech." Instead of Fareham, Waltham and Alresford, the bailiffs of the hundred of the bishop of Winchester, in which these three boroughs were situated, were informed. For Basingstoke, Alton and Andover, the hundreds of the same names were summoned (Hampshire) (P.W. I, 150, 35; 175, 42). Likewise Bedfordshire and Buckinghamshire (P.W. II, ii, 200, 51).

[3] P.W. I, 130, 59; compare P.W. II, iii, 348, 18.

[4] P.W. II, ii, 10, 27; compare P.W. II, iii, 380, 2, 3.

P.W. II, ii, 186, 10.

This slight and outward difference in the method of summoning had important consequences. It was natural that those towns which were summoned through the bailiffs of the hundreds easily found ways and means of freeing themselves from the burden of representation. Since this roundabout method led in any case to tardiness and neglect in this business, which had to be undertaken only once or twice a year, there was a temptation to arrange to be passed over by connivance, or in return for a small bribe, and this was so easy that it was often done. Thus it came about that the towns within hundreds, in by far the majority of counties, soon ceased, as a rule, to answer the summons, and therefore within a short time came to be passed over in the issuing of the summons. In Hampshire after 1311 the summoning of the boroughs that were parts of hundreds was given up altogether, and from then onwards only those towns that were on the same footing as the hundreds, and therefore were summoned by the sheriff direct, regularly received their summonses.[1]

On the other hand, in those more distant counties where the sheriff sent the writs of election direct to all the towns, the mayors less frequently disregarded these commands which had come in an extraordinary manner and from a far higher official, and especially because here corruption was more difficult, more dangerous, or even impossible. Conversely, under the sheriffs who chose an extraordinary method of summoning for the business of elections, fewer towns that ought to be summoned were left out; because they, the sheriffs, would cause the greater number of writs to be written and sent out according to a well-established list existing for this one purpose.

From this the following rules for the development of the summoning of the boroughs may be deduced, which hold good practically without exceptions.

---

[1] *P.W.* ii, ii, 66, 60, contains only the three abbreviations on the dorse: Wynton, Sutht, Portesm., for the three towns that were on a par with the hundreds, which also were the only ones represented. Likewise, *P.W.* ii, ii, 90, 47; 113, 52; 148, 73; 192, 28; 209, 73.

I

In the first place, all the towns that were on the same footing as hundreds, that is, those that on the other occasions had the *returnum omnium brevium* direct from the sheriff, were permanently summoned. According to the *Nomina Villarum* of 1316 (*P.W.* ii, iii, 301 ff.), these are Chichester, Arundel, Horsham, Steyning and Bramber, Lewes, Seaford and East Grinstead in Sussex; Southwark, Guildford, Reigate and Bletchingley in Surrey; Portsmouth, Southampton and Winchester in Hampshire; Wallingford, Reading and Windsor in Berkshire;[1] Norwich, Great Yarmouth and Lynn in Norfolk; Dunwich and Ipswich in Suffolk; Leominster and Hereford in Herefordshire; Canterbury and Rochester in Kent; Oxford in Oxfordshire; the city of Salisbury in Wiltshire; Bath in Somerset (*P.W.* ii, ii, 10); Exeter in Devon; Huntingdon in Huntingdonshire; Cambridge in Cambridgeshire; and Bedford in Bedfordshire.[2] Altogether in fifteen counties, thirty-four towns that were on a par with hundreds, that is, all the towns of that class, with the exception of Orford[3] in Suffolk, and Woodstock and Henley[4] in Oxfordshire.

II

Within the liberties, of course, only those places were to be summoned which, with regard to the bailiff of the liberty, had the *returnum brevium*, that is, their own administration. Here the roundabout way, through the bailiff of the liberty, was unavoidable, even in the more distant counties. Consequently

[1] [Windsor's inclusion in this list seems to be merely a slip, since on p. 31 Reiss adduces evidence for its being one of the towns within liberties.]

[2] To these must be added, according to note 3, p. 36, Gloucester and Bristol in Gloucestershire.

[3] This exception is to be explained by this town's consistent refusal of compliance. Till 1316 the summoning of Orford can almost always be traced in the abbreviations on the dorse (*P.W.* ii, ii, 49, 62, 108 are examples). But never did Orford allow itself to be represented. Therefore its name was struck out of the list of abbreviations (*P.W.* ii, 145) and never again included.

[4] With regard to Woodstock and Henley, the sheriff of Oxford himself stood in the way. Immediately at the first summons, he stated in his return that Oxford was the only borough of his bailiwick (*P.W.* i, 40, 24; 98, 30; etc.). Consequently Woodstock was represented only once (1302), Henley never.

the towns within liberties that were summoned dwindled to a very few.

In Suffolk, for example, the Villae Sancti Edmundi and Sanctae Etheldredae,[1] in the liberties of the same names, were regularly summoned till 1318 without their sending representatives. Then the sheriff ceased to inform the bailiffs of the liberties, and so the summonses of these places disappeared for ever.[2]

On the other hand, as a result of numerous representations, Wycombe in Buckinghamshire maintained its right to be summoned until the time of Edward III, although it was situated in the liberty of the honour of Wallingford and was summoned only indirectly through the bailiff of that liberty.[3]

Yorkshire contained a city and ten boroughs, but all of the last-named lay within liberties, so that the sheriff, in spite of the great distance from London, could not change to the direct summons. In consequence of this, we find, up to 1318, only one or two of these boroughs represented and that only occasionally, although, as a rule, more were summoned. Finally, after 1318, the two boroughs of Scarborough and Kingston-on-Hull were, with the city of York, regularly summoned,[4] apparently because they had become independent parts of the county, free from the bailiffs of the liberties.[5] Thus, with the single exception of Wycombe, all the towns within liberties lost their right to be summoned.

III

Likewise, in most counties, the summoning of towns within hundreds almost entirely disappears. In the more distant counties, however, which had gone over to the direct summon-

---

[1] [This passage raises a doubt as to whether Riess's explanation of the abbreviations is altogether satisfactory. There was no town of St Etheldreda and the only explanation that can be suggested for informing the bailiffs of the liberty is that the attendance of men of that liberty, perhaps of the bailiffs themselves, was desired for the county election. If Riess's theory as to the method of choosing the knights of the shire is correct, it may well have seemed important that the representatives of so great a landholder as the Prior of Ely should be present.]   [2] *P.W.* II, ii, 189, 21.

[3] *P.W.* II, ii, 200, 51.   [4] *P.W.* II, ii, 187, 201, 202, 301, 357.

[5] The city of York was, in 20 Richard II, raised to the status of a county and thereafter summoned direct from the chancery.

ing,[1] it continued as unimpaired as in the group discussed in section I. It survived in Buckinghamshire only for Wycombe[2] out of five towns; in Gloucestershire, only for Gloucester and Bristol,[3] whereas eight other boroughs lost their summonses.

On the other hand, in the counties which had advanced to direct summoning, almost all the towns remained parliamentary boroughs. In Somerset, there were four: Bridgewater, Taunton, Wells, Ilchester; in Dorset, seven: Dorchester, Lyme Regis, Melcombe, Shaftesbury, Wareham, Weymouth, Bridport;[4] in Devonshire, nine: Barnstaple, Plympton, Torrington, Totnes, Honiton, Sutton [Plymouth], Bradninch, Oakhampton, Tavistock; in Wiltshire, twelve (enumerated by Stubbs, *Constitutional History*, III, 449, n. 2); in Cornwall, six (Stubbs, *loc. cit.*). So we reach about thirty-eight towns within hundreds which, though they were not regularly represented, nevertheless retained the custom of being summoned.

According to this, the practice of summoning continued: 1, for the towns that were on the same footing as the hundreds; 2, for the towns belonging to hundreds in the counties of Wiltshire, Devon, Somerset, Dorset and Cornwall.

The summoning disappeared: 1, in the towns that were part of hundreds in the other counties; 2, in the towns that belonged to liberties.

[1] That Gloucestershire, in spite of its distance from London, did not give up the intermediation of the bailiffs of the hundreds, is proved by a dorsal abbreviation in *P.W.* II, ii, 143, "Grim." Grumbald's Ash is "Hundredum Regis". [There appears to have been no borough in the hundred of Grumbald's Ash. This strengthens the view expressed in my note on p. 35.]

[2] On p. 35 Wycombe is rightly described as lying within the honour of Wallingford.

[3] Bristol, after 50 Edward III, was summoned direct from the chancery and must therefore have previously risen to one of the towns that were on a par with the hundreds. Since we have a return of 1301 in which it is said: "Ceterum...breve returnatum fuit pro Burg. Bristol et Burg. Gloucester Ballivis libertatum Burgorum praedictorum qui habent returnum omnium brevium..." (for Bristol also *P.W.* II, 143), we may assume that in the *Nomina Villarum* of 1316 the sheriff had only forgotten to note the special position of these two boroughs before the others. It is better, therefore, to place Gloucester and Bristol in the first class.

[4] See the dorsal abbreviations, *P.W.* II, ii. 10.

CHAPTER III

The ACTIVE FRANCHISE *before* 1406, *especially in the* COUNTIES

THE investigation has now reached the point where we may ask: In what manner was the agreement on certain representatives reached in each electoral district? How was the right to representation of the administrative group shared among the numerous individuals contained within it?

We look especially for the idea that constituted the basis of this formally most important aspect of the representative system. Naturally, indeed, we look for this idea and its systematic development, in legislative acts or ordinances of the English kings; somewhat as in the Prussian state we find a legal regulation of these conditions in the constitutional documents, as in a series of complementary proclamations and laws.

The fact is, however, that during our whole period there is not to be found a single definition of what public services or what position in society should be required for the exercise of the right of election. So, then, this striking negative fact must be employed, as far as it is admissible, as a strong *argumentum ex silentio* to explain the matter. This has been done in full measure by Cox and Stubbs, and the question is only whether we can admit the validity of their conclusions.

Both these scholars are of the opinion that the English laws concerning elections in the Middle Ages rejected, in theory, all limitations of the right to vote; according to this the right of taking part in the choosing of the representatives of the country was consciously conceded to everyone. (Only it is held that this fundamental principle was not understood, or not accepted by those whom it concerned, and in practice was not carried out.[1]) In the abstract it is indeed possible that in mediaeval England such a general franchise was aimed at and officially recognized.

---

[1] Stubbs, *Constitutional History*, II, 228, 232.

But in our opinion this absence of definition could lead in-
evitably to a conclusion of such importance, or even form a
sufficient reason for it, only if, from a series of regulations
belonging together, this one restriction alone were absent,
showing a specific gap.[1] This, however, is altogether out of the
question, since adequate definitions are wanting with regard to
almost all aspects of the new institution.

Stubbs, to be sure, believes that he has found a positive confirmation of his theory in an answer of Edward III to a Commons'
petition of 1376, where it is said with regard to the representatives: "...q'ils soient esluz par commune assent de tout le
Countee". This, according to Stubbs, opposes that which the
commons demand, and expresses the force of an absolute general
right of election. It is therefore important for our investigation
to determine how this petition and its answer should be understood.[2] Now, the commons require something emphatically
negative: "the sheriffs shall not, under penalty, designate the
representatives of the counties without holding an election";
that is, they should not appoint members arbitrarily, but
should forward to the royal chancery the true result of an
election.

But to this is joined the positive requirement that the representatives shall be elected "par commune Election de les
meillours gentz des ditz Countees", that is, in my opinion, by a
common election two shall be chosen from among the best
people of the county. The point is, that the sheriff shall not
decide, but that the inhabitants of the county shall choose who
are to go to parliament as representatives. Clearly and certainly
the king decides in favour of the request, and against that which
was denounced, with the simple answer: "the knights of the
shire shall be chosen with the common assent of the whole
county". Whether here all inhabitants of the county, or only a

---

[1] With equal right one might conclude, for example, that in theory women
and children were also to take part in the elections since there is as little
definition of the age or sex of the individuals capable of voting.

[2] I give the petition here: "...Et que les Chivalers des Countees pur celles
Parlementz soient esluz par commune Election de les meillours Gentz des
ditz Countees; et nemie certifiez par le Viscont soul sans due Election, sur
certeine peyne. Answer: ...Et quant à l'article de l'Election des Chivalers qi
vendront a Parlement, le Roy voet, q'ils soient esluz par commune assen
de tout le Countee" (*Rot. Parl.* II, 355 a, 186).

certain group—particular classes—are in question, this bare phrase does not inform us.[1]

Let us then be content to lay it down that in our period qualifications for the franchise had not yet become the object of definition by legislation or in legal theory. Later we shall be able to utilize this significant fact for our investigation.

Since, therefore, a theory governing the right of election in our period is not to be ascertained, we shall have to consider all the more carefully the actual formation of this right.

From the well-established conditions and facts that are available for parliamentary elections, we shall set a limit to the number of possibilities that must be kept in mind; and finally from the particular conditions that appear in the various accounts of election procedure, from the forms in which the election business was carried out, we shall draw positive conclusions as to the class of persons who were concerned.

The most important questions are, How was the electoral

---

[1] Entirely different is the interpretation of Stubbs, who speaks of this petition five times (*Constitutional History*, II, 227, 433, 618; III, 400, 407). He construes "de les meillours Gentz" as a subjective genitive, thus making it apply to the electors, and sees as the object of the petition to open the elections to the higher social classes, but to exclude the lower. Accordingly the king's response appears to him as an entire refusal of the petition and the maintenance of the old condition that "everyone shall vote".

But the aim of the commons as well as that of the king would have had to be expressed quite differently and much more clearly for Stubbs to be right. Above all, there is not a trace of opposition between the petition of the commons and the answer. It already appears from this that the petitioners did not at all desire what Stubbs supposes and what would have been the exact opposite of that which the king decreed.

In order to reach full certainty, let us turn, for a comparison, to the statute concerning the election of coroners which is also presented by Stubbs as entirely analogous (*op. cit.* II, 227). The statute is from the year 1354, and thus only twenty-two years older: "Item, ordene est & establi q̃ touz Coroners des Countees soient esluz en pleins Contees, p les Cões de meismes les Contees, de plus loialx gentz q̃ s̃ront trovez es ditz Contees." Here, indeed, "esluz...par les Communites de mesmes les Contees" has the same meaning as the shorter "par commune Election" in our petition or the "esluz par commune assent de tout le Countee" of the answer, and "de plus covenables et plus loials gentz" corresponds exactly to the shorter "de les meillours Gentz" of our petition. After this comparison there can be no further doubt as to the correctness of the interpretation "from the best people".

All further assertions which Stubbs bases on his interpretation are, of course, also incorrect; e.g. *op. cit.* III, 406f.: "the petition shows that the election was often carried through in the absence of the better people of the county".

assembly in which the members were appointed constituted? How did it originate and what were the authoritative rules for it?

There is no doubt that the elections were always held in a regular meeting of the county court.[1] There it would be dealt with as an exceptional piece of business, arising by chance.[2] We must, therefore, try as carefully as possible to make clear to ourselves the position of the county court.

The County Courts

I

What was the business for which the inhabitants of the county came together?

(a) Judicial[3]

The county assembly attained exceptional importance as a court of law two or three times in the year, when the royal justices were present to exercise the criminal and higher civil jurisdiction.

The ordinary county assemblies before the sheriff were the places for numerous minor processes in which less than forty shillings was at stake.[4] Here, also, at the instance of individuals or of whole communities, a specially appointed commission (the grand jury) had to formulate the accusations, which would then be settled by a judicial decision before the royal justices.

But by no means all the minor processes had to be brought to the forum of the county court. A passage in Britton's Law Book shows clearly that the assemblies of the hundred, of the hamlet, of the liberty or of the vill[5] were also competent to deal with such processes. These courts would at all events have been resorted

---

[1] Already in the writ of election of 1226 it is said, expressly, that the election shall take place "in proximo comitatu tuo".

[2] Also Cox, *Antient Parliamentary Elections*, p. 83; Stubbs, *Constitutional History*, II, 225 f.; III, 404; Gneist, *Kommunalverfassung*, I, 241 and *Englische Verfassungsgeschichte*, p. 385.

[3] Cf. Gneist, *Englische Verfassungsgeschichte*, pp. 292-8.

[4] *Statutes of the Realm,*, I, 61, vi, Statutum Walliae, anno 1284.

[5] [This expansion of Britton's phrase "Courtz des frauncs hommes" into "versamlungen...des Hamlet, der Libertat, der Gemeinde" is misleading. If Britton meant more than the courts of liberties, he must have meant the Halmote or manorial court, as the hamlet and "Gemeinde" (which I have translated vill), as such, had no separate courts.]

to when both parties belonged to such a lower unit. Thus only the smaller number of the minor processes remained for the county court.[1]

(b) Administrative functions

These were of more importance to the inhabitants of the county, and were, indeed, also of wider scope. In the county court, those who were liable to the old feudal obligation of the landed proprietors, the receiving of the order of knighthood, were not only summoned to undertake this duty but were actually made to fulfil it.[2]

All general police regulations emanating from the royal chancery were made known in the county court.[3] Notice of the imposition of taxes which had to be raised within the ensuing months was given there; likewise complaints and grievances with regard to the collections were recorded and examined.[4]

That the election of the coroners should and did take place in this assembly we learn from the statute of Edward I: "We command that in the county court and with the assent of the county a coroner shall be elected";[5] as does also the confirmation by Edward III in 1354.[6]

From these casual examples, taken at random, it is clear that the county assembly was the place where a number of the important public affairs of the county were customarily discharged.

[1] Britton, *Treatise of Law*, ed. Nichols, I, 159, 8: "Et cum aucun se vodera pleyndre de acune dette de eynz la summe de xl. s. ou de acun petit trespas, en primes truysse pleges de sure sa pleynte al viscounte, si il vodera pleder en le Counté, ou a acun baillif, solom ceo qe il vodera pleder en hundredz ou en courtz des frauncs hommes;..." It is, indeed, almost unthinkable that the infinite number of minor processes could be settled in the thirteen days of the county court alone, especially as so much other business had also to be transacted there. [But some of the business of the county court was transacted in the *retro-comitatus* which was held on the following day (H. M. Cam, *The Hundred and the Hundred Rolls*, pp. 89, 107).]
[2] E.g. *P.W.* I, 214, 258.   [3] E.g. *P.W.* I, 376, 18.
[4] *P.W.* II, ii, 133, 57. [The reference here given is to knights' wages and is therefore irrelevant. The justices who were sent out to enquire into the conduct of the tax collectors may have held their investigations in the county courts, though it is not clear that they did so (J. F. Willard, *Parliamentary Taxes on Personal Property*, 1290 *to* 1334, pp. 219-29).]
[5] *Statutes of the Realm*, I, 62: "Rex vicecomiti salutem; Praecipimus tibi quod in pleno Comitatu tuo, & de assensu ejusdem Comitatus, eligi facias unum Coronatorem,"...
[6] *Statutes of the Realm*, I, 346, vi.

II

Recurrence of the County Courts

On this subject we can be quite clear.

Firstly, the meeting-place of the county assembly was permanently fixed. This is proved by the answer of Richard II to a complaint of the commons, that the royal justices held their sessions now here, now there: "The king commands that they hold their sessions in the principal towns in which the county courts are held."[1] Rightly, therefore, the commons of the county of Sussex complained under Edward II: "that no certain place is designated for the holding of the county court and that no place is appointed where the ordinances of the king must be made known". The king, thereupon, directed the sheriff to fix a place for both purposes.[2] Accordingly the same place in each county is always mentioned in the writs as the seat of the county court,[3] and in the new arrangements for the administration of Wales Edward I decreed: "and be it known, that the county court shall be held in the following manner, namely...in the place where the king will command".[4]

But was the time for the county court also fixed?

This question, too, is to be answered in the affirmative. For as often as, in the same county, the day of the week of the county

[1] *Rot. Parl.* III, 139, 40: "Le Roi le voet, q'ils [les Justices] tiegnent leur Sessions en les principalx & chiefs Villes, ou les Countees sont tenuz."

[2] *Rot. Parl.* I, 379, 73. The sheriff then appointed Chichester, as appears from a decree of Henry VII (*Statutes of the Realm*, II, 665, 24). [In the thirteenth century, the meeting-places for the county court of Sussex were Lewes and Shoreham. "The jurors of 1274 complained that Richard of Cornwall 'attracted' the county court to Chichester, to the grievous loss of the whole shire" (H. M. Cam, *The Hundred and the Hundred Rolls*, pp. 107–8). Chichester, however, continued to be a meeting-place, having, as Professor Morris has shown, "as many meetings as both of the others". "Subsequently Chichester became the sole meeting-place until the well-known statute of 19 Henry VII, cap. 29, prescribed that, in view of the hardship involved upon those who had to travel to the extreme end of the county, its court should meet alternately here and at Lewes" (W. A. Morris, *The Early English County Court*, p. 93, n. 22).]

[3] [There is evidence that in some counties, Sussex, Essex, Middlesex, Cornwall and perhaps others, the monthly assembly alternated between towns (Morris, *loc. cit.*; Cam, *loc. cit.*).]

[4] *Statutes of the Realm*, I, 56, iii: "Et sciendum quod hoc modo debet Comitatus teneri, scilicet...in loco ubi dominus Rex ordinaverit."

court is given or can be reckoned from the date, complete agreement is found: for Yorkshire, Monday; for Huntingdonshire, Saturday; for Rutland, Thursday, are three times given as the days of meeting. Again, the above-mentioned Statute of Wales only transferred to the conquered province an established practice when it further decreed: "and that is (the county courts shall be held) in one county on Monday, in another county on Tuesday, in a third on Wednesday, in a fourth on Thursday; and not on other days".[1]

Now I believe that every fourth Monday, or every fourth Wednesday, or Saturday, as the case might be, was the fixed and self-evident time for the county court of the different counties, and shall prove this from the few dates of the election returns.

For, if in each county whose election returns contain a note of the date at least twice, the dates of the county courts concerned are established, and if the time between each two county courts in the same county is reckoned, the number of the intervening days can regularly be divided by twenty-eight without a remainder.[2]

1. County courts of Somerset were held at Ilchester on:
   Monday, 12 November 1414.[3]
   Monday, 9 November 1417.[3]
   The difference amounts to 1092 days or 39 periods of four weeks.
2. For Yorkshire I have found the date noted three times:
   (a) Monday, 16 May 1412.[4]
   (b) Monday, 14 May 1414.[5]
   (c) Monday, 29 October 1414.[6]

---

[1] *Statutes of the Realm*, I, 56, 3: "et hoc per diem lune in uno Comitatu, per diem martis in alio comitatu, per diem mercurii in tertio comitatu, & per diem Jovis in quarto Comitatu, & non per alios dies".

[2] In order to obtain more examples I include here the period of the Lancastrians.

[3] Prynne, *Brevia Parliamentaria Rediviva*, III, 257, 258: "die lunae XII d. Nov. 2 Henry V" and "die lunae prox. ante festum Sancti Martini an. Regni Regis Henrici Quinti post conquestum quinto".

[4] *Ibid.* p. 152: "die Lune in festo Sancti Wilfridi, Episcopi", 13 Henry IV.

[5] *Ibid.* p. 153: "die Lune prox. ante festum Sancti Wilfridi Episcopi", 2 Henry V.

[6] *Ibid.* p. 268: "die lunae prox. ante festum omnium Sanctorum", 2 Henry V. [The meeting held on Monday, 29 October 1414, was the county court not of Yorkshire, but of the city of York, which by that time had been given the status of a county. This is shown by the words "in pleno Com. Civitatis Ebor'. tent. ibidem...".]

Between (*a*) and (*b*) there is a difference of 1008 days or 36 periods of four weeks; between (*b*) and (*c*) 168 days or 6 periods of four weeks.

3. For Huntingdonshire there are three dates:
    (*a*) Saturday, 16 October 1406.[1]
    (*b*) Saturday, 20 August 1429.[2]
    (*c*) Saturday, 17 October 1450.[3]

Between (*a*) and (*b*) there is a difference of 8344 days or 298 periods of four weeks; between (*b*) and (*c*) 7728 days or 276 periods of four weeks.

4. Three dates are given for Rutland:
    (*a*) Thursday, 26 December 1314.[4]
    (*b*) Thursday, 8 April 1322.[5]
    (*c*) Thursday, 21 October 1322.[6]

Between (*a*) and (*b*) there is a difference of 2660 days or 95 periods of four weeks; between (*b*) and (*c*) 196 days or 7 periods of four weeks.

5. There are two dates for Devon:
Saturday, 10 July 1311.[7]
Saturday, 18 January 1449.[8]

The difference between these two dates is 49,952 days or 1784 periods of four weeks.

6. Finally two dates are given for Northumberland:
Thursday, 22 September 1278.[9]
Thursday, 20 October 1449.[10]

Difference, 62,496 days or 2232 periods of four weeks.

Since all the pertinent cases from all the material that is available in print have been cited, this striking agreement cannot be due to mere chance. It is an indirect, but nevertheless a convincing, proof of the rule that exactly every four weeks a county court was held.[11]

---

[1] Prynne, *Brevia Parliamentaria Rediviva*, III, p. 253: "die Sabbati prox. post festum Sancti Dionysii", 8 Henry IV.

[2] *Ibid.* p. 273: "die Sabbati prox. ante festum sancti Barthi. Apostoli", 7 Henry VI.

[3] *Ibid.* p. 156: "die Sabbati prox. ante festum Sancti Lucæ Evangelistæ", 29 Henry VI.   [4] *P.W.* II, ii, 146, 69.

[5] *P.W.* II, ii, 255, 67.   [6] *P.W.* II, ii, 273, 48.   [7] *P.W.* II, ii, 46, 5.

[8] Prynne, *op. cit.* III, 253.   [9] *P.W.* I, 215.   [10] Prynne, *op. cit.* III, 168.

[11] [This discovery of Riess's appears to have been so entirely neglected that when Mr J. J. Alexander investigated the same points ("The Dates of Early County Elections", *E.H.R.* XL, 1–12 and "The dates of County Days",

From this it is clear that the day and place of the county court were, as a matter of course, sufficiently well known in the shires. A summons by the sheriff to the inhabitants of the county, as such, is out of the question, and, moreover, not the slightest indication of one is to be found.

This being so, not only does this point cease to be "obscure throughout"—as Stubbs[1] will have it, and Gneist,[2] following him, states—but also all speculations as to the possible arbitrariness of the summonses to the county court, which after all were only hypothetical, have no foundation.

III

Attendance at the county courts

With regard to this difficult question, I have been able neither to obtain a definite idea from the descriptions that have been given up to this time, nor to derive direct evidence from the material I have examined. Only a prudent realization of the determining factors can, considering the small amount of positive evidence, give us an impression which will be at all reliable.

Bulletin of the Institute of Historical Research, III, 89–95) his work was hailed as "establishing two new facts—that the county court met on definite days for each county, and that the courts were held at fixed intervals of twenty-eight or forty-two days" (W. C. Dickinson, "County Days in Scotland", *ibid.* p. 166). The only modification of Riess's view that Mr Alexander's articles render necessary is that in the counties of Northumberland, York, Lincoln and Lancaster, the interval between the meetings of the county court was six weeks. Riess himself might have observed that this was true, at least of Yorkshire, by closer attention to a document which he quotes in another connexion, where the phrase occurs: "ad comitatum Ebor. de sex septimanis in sex septimanas". The number of days which Riess quotes in discussing the county courts of Yorkshire and Northumberland can equally well be divided into periods of six weeks.

A further indication that the county courts were held at fixed times, which Riess has failed to notice, comes from a return made by the sheriff of Sussex in 1327: "Istud breve mihi venit in Comitatu Sussex' die Lune in vigilia Nativitatis beate Marie per quendam extraneum et nullus fuit Comitatus ante diem in brevi isto contentum tenendus et ideo electio militum nec breve istud ballivis civitatum et Burgorum pro brevitate temporis fieri non potuerunt. Et ideo de executione istius brevis nihil actum est ad presens" (*Return of Members of Parliament,* I, p. 79).]

[1] *Constitutional History,* III, 406.

[2] *Englische Verfassungsgeschichte,* p. 386.

Three points deserve to be emphasized:

1. The county courts were not closed and therefore were accessible to everyone who wished to take part in them. The proof of this lies, in the first place, in the *argumentum ex silentio*, that no indications of any surveillance of the persons who appeared are to be found. Then there is positive evidence from the later period, in which these conditions had become more important to contemporaries and have left for us some still discernible traces.

Thus we learn from a letter dated 15 November 1470 that one party intends to play the trick on its opponents of sending six or more armed men among them, in order to be able then to draw attention to the presence [in the court] of thievish persons without means of support.[1] This plan must have depended on the supposition that at that time a control of the persons who appeared was not yet exercised.

In 18 Henry VI (1439) the first electoral assembly had "quibusdam certis de causis" failed to come to an agreement; in order that the same thing might not happen when the second attempt was made at the next county court, the king ordered that "it should be made known publicly in the county court that no one in arms or in warlike apparel should proceed to the election".[2] When, even at so late a time, and even in such an important case, there is no talk of closing the county court against armed or unarmed rabble, our assumption with regard to the earlier period stands beyond a doubt.

2. But if we enquire what the average county court was like, it is only with difficulty that an answer can be deduced from the available material.

In our period, attendance at the county court was no longer a duty enforceable, and, in individual cases, enforced by police power. Only in response to a special summons must everyone appear. But, partly from the very varied interests in the business to be expected there, partly from the moral attractions of an honourable local patriotic activity in the presence of the assembled

---

[1] *Paston Letters*, II, 56, 57.
[2] *Rot. Parl.* V, 7, 18: "...publice in eodem Comitatu proclamari..., ne aliqua persona tunc ibidem armata seu modo guerrino arraiata ad electionem illam accedat...". See also *Statutes of the Realm*, II, 170, 1.

neighbourhood, a fairly numerous and, on the whole, constant attendance of the inhabitants of the county may be assumed.

By the Statute of Marlborough the great lords were allowed to appear in the county courts by representatives. From a later period, at least, we have evidence as to the way in which this representation took place. In 13 Henry IV, for Yorkshire, seven attorneys are mentioned by name with their principals, with the note that they are appointed substitutes for this year. Three years later, others are nominated for the same magnates.[1] It seems therefore that participation in the county court was far from being taken too lightly.

That, beside the knights, the freeholders were especially numerous requires no further proof.

With regard to the villeins, the small peasants, attendance at the county court had never had the force of a duty. Whereas the directions for making the *extenta manerii*—attributed to 4 Edward I—say, concerning the freeholders, "it is to be enquired, with regard to the free tenants, who owe suit from one county court to another, and who do not",[2] a similar requirement is not to be found in the rules for the registration of the *Customarii* and *Coterelli*, in spite of their agreement on other points.

But that the villeins were not only allowed to attend the county courts, but were customarily employed in its business, appears from the proviso, unimportant in itself, which is attached to their unassailable participation as jurors: that the permission of the lord was necessary if the parties claimed it.[3]

Women and children could indeed, or must, at times, have been attendants at the county court on account of the processes in which they were concerned; there is evidence of the presence of ecclesiastical persons; but these elements were, of course, of no significance. Far more important is the circumstance that in the county court those who belonged to other counties could appear and that probably numerous burgesses from the towns within the county were regularly present. For these were

---

[1] Prynne, *Brevia Parliamentaria Rediviva*, III, 152f.
[2] *Statutes of the Realm*, I, 242: "Inquirendum est de praedictis libere tenentibus & qui secuntur Curiam de Comitatu in Comitatum & qui non...."
[3] Britton, *Treatise of Law*, ed. Nichols, I, 209.

inhabitants of other electoral districts and had already taken part in the appointment of their own representatives.

The importance of this incongruity must not be under-estimated; because the county court itself was almost always held within another constituency of this kind—a borough—and for that reason, as may be assumed *a priori*, was particularly largely attended by the inhabitants of this alien electoral district.

3. It is now desirable to estimate the attendance at the county court. Gneist has in mind "a very small number" and speaks of "a few who happened to be present".[1] The opposite opinion would be nearer to the truth.

It seems to me that the assumption, to be proved later, that the sureties for the appearance of the members were appointed from among the attendants at the county court,[2] is of service here. For it happened often enough that the same persons were repeatedly elected members, and then, almost always, they had the same sureties. This proves surely that, for the better classes of the population, attendance at the county court was fairly regular, and not dependent on their particular needs.

But, above all, I wish to introduce the numerical evidence that is attainable in support of this view.

On 26 June 1278, it was commanded that all holders of twenty pounds' worth of land and more who had not already assumed the order of knighthood, should be admonished to do so before Christmas. On 22 September 1278, the sheriff executed this order for Northumberland in the county court. It concerned forty men; each appointed four sureties, and two as many as six, but since seventeen names are repeated we meet only 109 different sureties: altogether 149 persons who are mentioned by name.[3] From this number of well-to-do persons who attended it may be inferred that the number of all those who were present was much higher.[4]

[1] *Englische Verfassungsgeschichte*, pp. 386, 387.
[2] Cf. Appendix II.
[3] [I have carefully re-examined this list and it shows that some of the men who had to find pledges were themselves sureties for others. In all twenty-two names are repeated, but as some are repeated more than once these twenty-two account for fifty-five of the names. Thus the total number of persons is 171.]
[4] *P.W.* I, 214.

In the county court of Lincoln an oath was taken by 21 knights, 330 other inhabitants, 13 burgesses of Stamford, 8 of Grantham, 22 of Lincoln, 23 of Grimsby: altogether 417 persons whose names are given. It is expressly stated that only the more important and substantial men of the county and only the officials of the subordinate districts and towns were sworn.[1]

Finally, in 1450, 494 electors in Huntingdonshire are enumerated. When it is considered to what a narrow circle of those who were entitled to appear in the county court the right of voting was then restricted (even though allowance must be made for the influence of interest in the election), a larger number is nevertheless reached.

We must, therefore, picture the attendance at the county courts as uneven, but always comprising from 500 to 1000 persons.

When, after this digression, we now return to the main course of the investigation, and actively pursue the end in view, we must, in order to be able to attain that end, first consider the general principal factors in their full significance.

1. The full force of our *argumentum ex silentio*, discussed above, now appears. Since the most varied classes of the population were together in the county court, if any restriction of the franchise had been considered necessary, it would have had to be proclaimed. The full positive significance of the fact that this step was not found necessary now reveals itself.

2. There is no trace of the constitution of an electoral assembly, although, as has been shown above, representatives of other constituencies (the boroughs) were regularly present and the county court was entirely accessible to everyone.

The positive evidence for this is to be obtained by retrospective inferences from the following period. In the year 1439, by which time repeated statutes had quite clearly defined the classes of persons authorized to vote, an election in Cambridgeshire, as we have seen above, "certis de causis" did not take

---

[1] *Rot. Parl.* III, 400: "Nomina generosiorum et validiorum hominum Comitatus Lincoln', necnon Majorum, Ballivorum et Aldermannorum ejusdem Comitatus, qui coram Anketillo Mallore, ac Vicecomite Lincoln' Sacramentum praestiterunt."

place. In order that, at the holding of the new election, the same hindrances might not recur, the king issued special precautionary measures: by a proclamation, everyone who was not qualified should be commanded to abstain from interfering in the act of electing, and "not to give his vote"; those who contravened this should be severely punished.[1] That in this particularly urgent case not even a real method of constituting the assembly, but only a makeshift substitute for one is suggested, is a sufficient proof that the lack of any traces of a constitution is due to the absence of the thing itself.

3. Moreover, one must not overlook the fact that the elections in the different counties took place on different days. For with the openness of the county courts, and in the absence of any act by which the electoral assembly was constituted before the beginning of this business, particularly interested persons could well take part in elections in different counties.

4. Finally, it should be observed that it would not previously be made known that an election was on the agenda for the next county court, so that the inhabitants of the county could not previously have been occupied in considering their interests, in conferring beforehand and in concerting measures.[2] With this lack of assured forms and of arrangements imposed from without, it must be admitted that an election contest, a rational method of giving legal expression to divergent interests and aims, is utterly unthinkable.

Now when in 105 years about 8000 elections took place without the chancery's receiving numerous complaints and protests against the abuse of these loose forms in favour of the victorious

[1] *Rot. Parl.* v, 7, 18 (16 November 1439): "...quod ipse, [Vicecomes]... in proximo comitatu suo,...antequam ad hujusmodi electionem faciendam procedat, publice in eodem Comitatu proclamari & inhiberi faciat, ne aliqua persona tunc ibidem armata seu modo guerrino arraiata ad electionem illam accedat, nec quicquam quod in perturbationem pacis ipsius Domini Regis, seu electionis illius cedere valeat, ibidem vel alibi faciat vel attemptet, nec quod aliqua persona se de electione illa aliqualiter intromittat, nec vocem suam in electione illa, ea tantummodo excepta persona que vocem in hujusmodi electione infra Comitatum predictum faciendum, juxta forman Statuti in eodem Brevi specificatam, habere debeat, dare presumat quovis modo,...." For a similar case see *Paston Letters*, II, 56 (15 November 1470).
[2] [If, as Riess himself has shown, below, p. 53, the magnates or their stewards might be specially summoned for an election, the fact that one was to be held cannot have been altogether unknown in the county.]

party,[1] when, on the other hand, in the following period group interests are introduced, as from without, into the elections and also a legal establishment of the election procedure was attempted (in the most primitive forms, as we shall see), there can, in my opinion, be no doubt that in our period neither the need nor the intention existed to ascertain, through the electoral procedure, the weight of the different opinions and interests within the county.

If we dwell for a moment on the inner causes of this phenomenon, two reasons, which are self-evident, are entirely sufficient to explain it: 1, the aim and duties (competence) of the representation of the country as they have been disclosed in Chapter 1; 2, the simple conditions of a population living by agriculture and cattle-breeding (the towns were indeed excluded), where interests were naturally very similar and far from being concerned with political oppositions.

But where tension in society is lacking, where strong political motives touching existence itself do not play a part, a more developed form and method of the contest cannot be reached.

Not until we have entirely eliminated all these possibilities which we are accustomed *a priori* to associate with an election of the representatives of the country can we, as a result of the concentration of our thought within these limits, think of obtaining from the existing material what is positively correct and was once actual.

With an unprejudiced reading everything comes to two points, which may well exist together:

I. The election should be made and was made with unanimity. Thus we take the words of Edward III's ordinance of 1376,[2] "q'ils soient esluz par commune assent de tout le Countee", in their full meaning: "by common assent of the whole county court".

The like is said in countless sheriffs' returns; we give some variations from the time of Edward I: "by the assent of the aforesaid county court",[3] "by virtue of the assent of the whole

---

[1] That the few surviving complaints have an entirely different significance will appear below.

[2] See above, p. 38.

[3] *P.W.* I, 59, 27: "ex assensu praedicti Comitatus."

county court of Devon...",[1] "in the county court of Dorset
by the whole community of the same county "[2]. "In the county
court of Gloucestershire, I have caused to be elected...with
the assent of the same county court...".[3] "The whole county
court of Middlesex has elected".[4]

To the effects of this requirement on the holding of an
election, I shall presently return.

II. But how were the candidates found who could then be
elected by common assent?

Naturally thus; one or several of the most considerable men
of the county would propose two suitable persons.

This I infer from a complaint which Matthew de Cranthorn
presented in the year 1319 and which says: "When a writ came
to the county court of Devonshire for sending to this parliament
two knights for the community of the said county, he, the same
Matthew, had been chosen by the Bishop of Exeter and Sir
William Martin and with the assent of the other good men of
that county."[5]

Thus the election was decided: 1, by the two men who can be
identified as the greatest landholders of the county,[6] and, 2, by
the assent of all the others. This admits of no other interpretation than that these two had proposed Matthew as a candidate,
and thus had performed the important act that must precede
every acclamation.

Now when in a return for Oxfordshire and Berkshire of the
time of Edward II, besides the abbreviations for the towns, a

---

[1] *P.W.* I, 67, 10: "de assensu totius Comitatus Devon'."

[2] *P.W.* I, 68, 11: "in pleno Comitatu Dorset per totam communitatem
ejusdem Comitatus."

[3] *P.W.* I, 94, 19: "Eligi in pleno Comitatu Gloucester' feci...per assensum
ipsius Comitatus."

[4] *P.W.* I, 72, 23: "Totus Comitatus Middlesex elegerunt."

[5] *P.W.* II, ii, Appendix, 138, 41: "...que come briefs fust venuz en le
Conte de Deveneshire pur faire venir ici a cest parlement deus Chivalers
pur la commune del dist Conte meime celuy Matheu par le Evesque de
Excestre, Sire Williame Martyn, par assent des autres bone gentz de cel
Conte, si fust elu...". Stubbs, *Constitutional History*, III, 421, has entirely
misunderstood this complaint.

[6] The Bishop of Exeter was lord of the hundreds of Crediton and Bampton;
William Martyn can be identified as the lord of the hundreds of Braunton,
Fremington and South Molton. According to the *Nomina Villarum*, no
other had equally large possessions. Thus these two are indeed the most
important persons in the county.

dorsal abbreviation of the following is jotted down: "execution, to summon the magnates or their stewards for the choosing of the knights",[1] I infer that the sheriff had wanted to secure the presence of suitable persons for the nomination of the candidates.

In this sense we can best explain the answer given by the sheriff of Sussex in 1297: "I had the knights and landholders of the county of Sussex come before me. But in the absence of the Archbishop of Canterbury and other persons (bishops, earls, barons, knights and others) they would not undertake the election of representatives."[2] Thus, although knights and freeholders were present, no election took place because these most important men, who were accustomed by nominating the candidates to bear the principal part in the election, were absent.

We have also more direct evidence as to the method of nomination. In a number of returns the names of those elected are first merely noted, and then in the return itself repeated in an orderly manner with their sureties. Here, I believe, the sheriff had at first noted the candidates who were suggested to him; then asked the assembly for its assent, and finally, when this had been given, made out the election return.[3]

The best corroborative evidence for this assumption is yielded by two returns in which a name, so jotted down, has been crossed out and another put in its place.[4] On the back of a writ of election for Devon is to be found "the return to this writ is on an (attached) slip".

Jacobus de Oxton.
Nicholas de Alneto. † ~~Will de fferrers~~ †

On the slip then is the detailed return of Nicholas de Alneto and James de Oxton. From this it appears that William de fferrers, one of the two candidates who had been named, had been refused the necessary common assent, so that a new candidate had

---

[1] *P.W.* II, ii, 272, 47   ex[ecutio]
"ad venir̄[e] fac̄[iendum] Magnates vel eorum señ[escallos] pr[o] Militibus elig̃[endis]."
[2] *P.W.* I, 60, 36.
[3] E.g. *P.W.* I, 70, 16:
 (Hertford' 25 May, 1298.)
  "Milites"
  "Joh. Ayngnel" } the names are repeated in the return.
  "Robts de Hoo" }
Likewise *P.W.* I, 119, 23; II, ii, 108, 42; 205, 66; 253, 63; 275, 51.
[4] *P.W.* II, ii, 142, 52.

to be nominated and noted by the sheriff. Since he was more fortunate, the sheriff could then draw up his report.[1]

We now come back to the consequences of point 1.

The whole force of the method of election, with unanimity as an essential requirement, is on the negative side, the slightest opposition immediately putting an end to any candidature. I believe that, in fact, the expressed opposition of one or more persons present was, in this sense, decisive.

Certainly there lay in this a great danger that the election might not take place at all; a danger which was the greater, the more open and more frequented the county court. But at this point we see not only tradition but also definite precepts of royal statutes affording protection: "It is provided that the sheriff shall allow no small, insignificant man to speak in the County court."[2]

So supported, the sheriff could disregard the opposition of an unimportant individual inhabitant of the county, whenever it was uttered; but the expressed opposition of a more influential person, or the united declaration of several opponents of good reputation, would necessitate his crossing out of the candidate that we have observed above.

There are a petition and a complaint which are of great service to us in showing the strict enforcement of this principle.

On Tuesday, 17 November 1392, "Philip Courtenay, who had been named in the sheriff of Devon's return as one of the

---

[1] Similarly, *P.W.* II, ii, 147:

Somerset and Dorset.

Joh. de Cerne.

Johes de Wroxhale.

[2] *Statutes of the Realm*, I, 35, Statutum Westm. prim. c. 33, Anno 1275: "Purveu est que nul Visconte ne seoffre baretour meintenir paroles en Conte...." [The passage will not bear this interpretation. The word barrator means one who causes strife, or incites to litigation, and is not descriptive of social position. That it was used in its ordinary sense here seems clear from the context: "Purveu est que nul Visconte ne seoffre baretour meintenir paroles en Conte; ne Seneschaus de grant Seygnurs, ne autre sil ne seit attorne son Seygnur a suite fere ne rendre les Jugemenz des Contez ne pronuncier les Jugemenz, sil ne seit especialment prie & requis de ceo fere de tuz les suitiers e les attornez des suitiers qui i serront a la Jorneie;...." The aim of the statute was apparently to prevent persons who were not suitors to the county court, whatever their rank, from influencing its proceedings. The fact that the stewards of great lords were considered specially likely to do this shows clearly that barrators were not expected to be "small insignificant men".]

knights for the said county", came before the king in parliament and said: "that he had learned that certain persons had as well in writing as by word of mouth accused and slandered him of odious things to the King and Lords. And he prayed, therefore, to be released from the said duty until the said matters of complaint and grievances had been investigated and found to be true or false...and since the said petition seemed right to the King and the Lords, the King granted his request....And afterward because he showed himself to be good and reasonable towards those who had brought complaints against him and came to a good understanding with them, he was, in full parliament, restored to his good fame."[1]

From this it appears that Philip Courtenay regarded it as proper to lay down his mandate until the matter in dispute should have been decided and that the king as well as the parliament shared his opinion. Even the official who made the record expressed himself remarkably vaguely and cautiously: "who in the return was named as one of the members for the said county". Naturally the election seemed to him, on account of the subsequent opposition of two persons,[2] to be imperfect, so that he had to paraphrase the usual simple title.

But why did not these opponents make their opposition effective at the right time in the electoral assembly, and by their dissent prevent his election? This question which, after our previous explanation, is so obvious, the complainants have not omitted to answer, in anticipation, in their complaint. They

---

[1] "...Philipp Courtenay, q'estoit retournez par le Viscont de Devenshire un des Chivalers pur la dite Counte,...en disant, Coment il avoit entenduz, q̃ certeines Gentz luy avoient accusez & esclaundrez au Roi & as Seigneurs, si bien par bille come par bouche, des heynouses maters; & sur ceo pria d'estre deschargez de la dit occupation tan q̃ les ditz accusementz & compleintz furent triez & trovez vrais ou nient vrais. Et a cause q̃ sa dite priere sembla au Roi & as Seigneurs honeste, le Roi luy ettroia sa requeste.... Et puis apres, a cause q'il avoit este bon & tretable ovesque ceux q̃ firent compleintz sur luy, & condescendu(t) a bone treite, il fuist restitut en plein Parlement a sa bone fame" (*Rot. Parl.* III, 300, 6).

[2] [The Rolls of Parliament, the only authority cited by Riess for this incident, mention only certain persons; but he is, apparently, right in giving the number as two. "The accusations were made by Thomas Pontingdon, whom Courtenay had expelled from the Manor of Bickleigh, and by Richard Somestre, whom he had expelled from four marks of land in Thorverton" (J. J. Alexander, "Devon County Members of Parliament", *Trans. Devon Association*, XLV, 254).]

state that Philip Courtenay was so powerful that no poor man could pursue his rights against him or speak without hesitation in the county court.[1] Formally, then, it had been in the power of the two complainants to compel the choosing of another.

A second case is somewhat less clear. According to a return of January 1324, Gilbert de Haydok was elected for Lancashire;[2] but in his place Thomas de Lathum appeared in parliament, as is shown by the writ *de expensis*.[3] This striking and altogether unusual phenomenon is to be explained by a process before the grand jury of Derby[4] on 29 September 1323;[5] there it was complained against a former sheriff that he had sent to the parliament of 6 to 25 October 1320[6] Gilbert de Haydok and another member, who received four shillings a day, whereas otherwise only two shillings was customary in this county.[7]

This error of nearly three years before was, at any rate, only pointed out after and probably as a consequence of Haydok's re-election, by an inhabitant of the county—perhaps at the next county court, and as a result of careful investigation. But even the subsequent censure of a regularly elected person seems to have sufficed to render a new appointment necessary. The thing itself was only decided when the itinerant justices were next present.

We are, then, of the opinion that in these two cases even subsequent opposition was sufficient to endanger the validity

---

[1] *Rot. Parl.* III, 302, 14: "Et le dit Monsieur Philipp est si grant en pais, q̃ null povere homme n'ose envers luy son droit pursuir, ne nul homme encontre luy verite dire."   [2] *P.W.* II, 303, 66.
[3] *P.W.* II, ii, 312, 85.   [4] [West Derby in Lancashire.]
[5] *P.W.* II, ii, 315, 89; also printed by Cox, *Antient Parliamentary Elections*, p. 85.   [6] The date is found in *P.W.* II, ii, 229.
[7] This is to be found by calculations from *P.W.* II, ii, 258, 75, and elsewhere. [This is an inaccurate version of the charge, which was that the sheriff had returned the two members without holding an election and that if the inhabitants of the county had been allowed to choose their representatives, they could have obtained suitable men who would have served for ten marks or ten pounds instead of the twenty pounds that Haydock and his colleague had required. "Et quod cum quoddam breve Regis venisset eidem *Willielmo* pro duobus militibus eligendis ad eundum ad parliamentum Regis qui eligi debuissent per totam communitatem Comitatus idem *Willielmus* elegit *Gilbertum de Haydok* et *Thomam de Thorntone* sine assensu communitatis qui cum redissent de Parliamento tulerunt breve pro expensis suis levandis per quod praeceptum fuit praedictis Ricardo et Willielmo de Wynwyk Ballivis quod levarent *xx. libras* pro expensis praedictorum militum ubi communitas istius Comitatus habuisse potest de electione sua propria duos sufficientes homines ad eundum ad parliamentum pro *x. marcis* vel *x. libris*" (*P.W.* II, ii, 315, 89).]

of an election. In them the strict necessity for unanimous agreement of all the inhabitants of the county seems to be carried to the highest point.

It is obvious that with this rule for the act of electing, the possibility of abuse was abundantly given and was close at hand. Let us make clear to ourselves the form this would take, for nothing shows the nature and force of a comprehensive rule better than the provisions for exceptions and departures therefrom. The possibilities of abuse which Gneist and Stubbs suppose[1] have already been shaken;[2] now, they appear entirely to fall to the ground. Since of what possible use was it for the sheriff (if for a moment we concede the case) to summon some of his friends and to leave his opponents uninformed, if even a few opponents were sufficient to defeat his scheme? But according to our presentation, we can admit only two methods of influencing the election, and of fraud by the sheriff, which could affect the result. 1, If the candidates who had been proposed and confirmed by acclamation were unsatisfactory to him, he could, later, on empty pretexts, find manucaptors for others and give them in his return. 2, He himself could propose two candidates, or have them proposed by his friends, without submitting to the test of the general acclamation at all, or, if dissent were expressed, without having regard to it. These two cases are the only ones in which illegality was possible and which were formally impeachable. The first is the making of false returns, the second, the neglect of the *communis assensus*.

If now we examine the surviving reports of irregularities in the elections, they are found to fall neatly under these two headings.

1. Evidence of false returns. The above-mentioned record of Matthew Cranthorn complained further, "but in deception of him (Cranthorn) Robert Beudyn, the sheriff of the said county had, in his return, designated another instead of him against the will of the said community".[3] As a matter of fact, the person who was guilty, the undersheriff, was thus made to answer "for the false return".

---

[1] *Constitutional History*, III, 406 ff.   [2] *Supra*, p. 45.

[3] *P.W.* II, ii, Appendix, 138, 41: "Mes ore en deceite de luy, Robert Beudyn, Visconte del dist Conte si ad retourne autres en son lyeu encontre la volunte de dist commune...." Endorsed: "Quoad istam peticionem, habeat Breve Thes. & Baron. de Scaccario, quod venire fac. Subvicecomitem ad respondendum de falso returno praedicto."

In 7 Richard II, Shaftesbury presented a complaint that it had elected two representatives, but that "Monsieur John Stretch, the sheriff of Dorset, had returned a certain Thomas Cammel, contrary to the will of the underwritten mayor and communalty".[1]

Finally, when in the parliament of 1403 complaint was made "that the election return sent in by the sheriff of Rutland was insufficient and not in accordance with his duty",[2] the sheriff and William de Oudeby, whom he had returned, were summoned, as was also Thomas de Thorp, "who had been chosen, in full county court, to be one of the representatives of the same county and nevertheless was not designated in the return by the said sheriff". Judgement was given "that he (the sheriff) should correct the same return and therein designate the said Thomas as one of the representatives, as he had been chosen in the said county court".[3]

2. Against the other form of abuse, the neglect of the test as to unanimity, the above-mentioned Commons' petition of 1376 was especially directed: "...that the representatives of the counties should never be designated by the sheriff alone without due election".

But as early as the reign of Edward II, it was the subject of a complaint that two sheriffs, "without the assent of the community", had chosen the representatives "who ought to have been elected by the whole community of the county".[4]

---

[1] Prynne, *Brevia Parliamentaria Rediviva*, III, 286: "...Monsieur John Stretch, Viscount de Dors[et]...retorna un Thomas Camel,...encontre la volunte des Maire & Com[mu]nes susdites...."

[2] *Rot. Parl.* III, 530, 38: "Item, por ce q̃ le Brief de Somons de Parlement retourne p le Viscont de Roteland ne feust pas sufficientement ne duement retournee,...."

[3] *Rot. Parl.* III, 530, 38: "Et sur ce les ditz Seigñrs firent venir devant eux en Parlement, si bien le dit Viscont, come William Ondeby qui feust retourne p le dit Viscont pur un des Chivalers du dit Countee (thus the same expression as on p. 55, n. 1), & Thomas de Thorp qi feust esluz en plein Countee d'estre un des Chivalers de mesme le Countee pur le dit Parlement, & nient retourne p le dit Viscont....agardez est...por ce q̃ le dit Viscont n'ad fait sufficientement son Retourne du dit Brief, q'il amende mesme le Retourne, & q'il retourne le dit Thomas pur un des ditz Chivalers, come il feust eslu en le dit Countee...." The removal of the sheriff followed.

[4] *P.W.* II, ii, 315, 89: "...Et quod cum quoddam breve Regis venisset eidem Willo [Henrico] pro duobus Militibus eligendis ad eundum ad parliamentum Regis, qui eligi debuissent per totam communitatem Comitatus, idem Willus elegit...sine assensu communitatis...."

Lastly, when in 1406 a complaint was directed against "the illegal election of knights of the shire", and which explains in more detail that they were sometimes appointed according to the whim of the sheriff, contrary to "the wording of the writs addressed to the said sheriffs", this can only mean that the *Communitas Comitatus* had not been given its right; that its *communis assensus* had not been obtained.

Thus the only persons who exercised real influence, whose participation was decisive in the business of the election, were: 1, the most important men of the county, especially inasmuch as they proposed the candidates; 2, those inhabitants of the county of good reputation who were sufficiently independent and courageous to give their veto against a candidate.

In a formal sense indeed, and in the outward act, the inferior persons who were present in the county court could also participate. They might well support an expressed veto, or assent to an accomplished unanimous election, and indeed imagine that this was only a modest exercise of a really higher right. But we find no traces of the slightest influence by the great mass of the people; and the circumstance that success continued for so long without legal rules can only be explained by the fact that these classes saw no occasion, and felt no desire, to play a decisive part in the elections.

The election of the Borough Members

In this province, too, previous research has not yet reached results that can stand the test of a stricter investigation.[1]

The different acts by which every borough election was accomplished must be kept strictly apart and examined separately.

1. The bailiffs of the borough received from the sheriff instructions to provide for the representation of their district in

[1] Gneist, *Englische Verfassungsgeschichte*, p. 385, sums up the conclusions of Stubbs as follows: "The formal (!) election of the members for the towns took place in the county court, and the names of the representatives were given in the same writ which dealt with the election of the county knights.... Probably (!) the deputations from the different boroughs either announced to the sheriff the names of those whom they had chosen in an election made on the spot, or reported the result of one that had previously been held in the town meeting. The latter was probably (!) the rule in towns whose constitutions were at all developed."

parliament. In almost every election return is to be found "et breve illud returnatum fuit ballivis villae" or a similar phrase.

2. That the result of the election for the towns was also recorded and sent into chancery likewise by the sheriff is indubitable, and has been accepted by Stubbs and Gneist.

But the question is, in what manner was the answer given to the sheriff, from which he could transcribe what was necessary in his return.

The answer to this too cannot be in doubt. For, in the returns, before the names of the borough representatives are given (in all the innumerable cases), it is always said, "the bailiffs have answered so and so" (never "the deputies", never "the burgesses"), or what is even more convincing—when towns that have received a summons remain unrepresented, it is said "the bailiffs have given me no answer".[1] Thus the sheriff always received and expected information direct from the bailiffs.

But with this the two probabilities which Stubbs and Gneist have in mind are irreconcilable; for otherwise, in so vast a number of cases, there must be, at least once, some such phrase as "no deputation has appeared" or "the deputies assert that they have received no commission" or the like. But this is not so.

We must, of course, assume that the bailiffs gave their response in writing, and sent it by their usual messengers to the sheriff, who then used it for the composition of his return and kept it as a record for himself. Most convincing evidence for this procedure comes from two responses which a sheriff, contrary to custom, once sent in along with his return.[2]

---

[1] E.g. *P.W.* I, 150, 33: "...et iidem ballivi nullum michi inde dederunt responsum", and also in countless other cases.

[2] *P.W.* II, ii, 200, 51: "Ego Philippus de Ailesbury (we have already met him as an exceptionally painstaking official, *supra*, p. 25) Vicecomes Bed' et Buk' ad istud breve sic respondeo:...Pro burgo de Bedeford feci returnum istius brevis Willo de Catteworthe et Stephano de Bole, Ballivis libertatis Burgi praedicti,...qui michi respondent prout patet in indentura huic brevi consuta. Et pro burgo de Wycombe......sicut patet in quadam alia indentura huic brevi consuta." The attached indentures begin,

I, for Bedford: "Philippo de Aylesbury, vicecomiti...Wilhelmus de Catterworth et Stephanus le Bole, ballivi libertatis villae Bedford...respondent...."

II, for Wycombe: "Philippo de Alusbury, Vicecomiti,...per Radulphum de Brehull, Ballivum honoris Walingford sic responditur de Burgensibus de Wicoumbe...."

Similarly, *P.W.* II, ii, 143, 55, for Bristol.

Only a doubt may still be raised by those who wish to hold to, at least, some part of Stubbs's theory, as to whether the deputies of the town to the county court, concerning whom we have abundant evidence for the twelfth century, were not later employed in the business of transmitting the return. Owing to the remarkable importance of quite accidental formalities in the development of English constitutional life, we must by no means neglect to make clear to ourselves this matter of their service as messengers.

But if this had been the custom the sheriff could have received the responses only on the day of the county court itself, never earlier, never later. Since he could only begin his return after the conclusion of the election of the county members on that day, the responses would always have been in his hands in good time.

It can be shown, however, that very often the sheriff did not receive the responses until after the composition of his return. When, for example, he states that such and such a town has not replied, whereas it is, in fact, represented in parliament, we have such a case of a delayed response.[1] Moreover, in a return for Yorkshire, the full statement that Scarborough had sent no answer is entirely struck out, and, further down, the contents of the response, which had arrived later, with the names of those elected is given.[2]

From this it is obvious that the written answer could be and very often was communicated to the sheriff outside of the county court. And herewith the last remains of the "formal election in the county court", which Stubbs and Gneist have supposed, disappear.

It will be admitted that these matters which appear so superficial and paltry are, nevertheless, the most important points for the reconstruction of the course of the borough elections.

They prove, contrary to the prevailing opinion, that the appointment of the two burgesses was arranged entirely within

---

[1] E.g. Colchester, 23 February 1305, *P.W.* I, 143, 18; 157, 47.

[2] *P.W.* II, ii, 46, 6: "Quoad venire faciendum duos Burgenses de Burgo de Skardeburgh,... qui nullum inde michi dedit responsum" is crossed out, but there follows: "Nomina Burgencium Ville de Skardeburgh N.N." Also the sheriff of Berkshire (25 Henry VI) wrote to the mayor and bailiffs of Windsor, that they should hold an election and have the answer sent to him: "cum omni possibili festinatione in villa de Abingdon indilate" (Prynne, III, 292).

the town, and as a domestic affair of the community. The bailiffs of the town made out the certificate as to the result of the election and sent it at a convenient time to the sheriff so that he could embody it in his return.[1]

Now if we enquire about the rules according to which the elections took place in the boroughs, the sheriff's returns show three different forms of election procedure.

1. The bailiffs appointed two members according to their own judgement; thus, for example, it is said in two returns for Northampton, "the bailiffs themselves have chosen".[2]

2. The bailiffs summoned a number of prominent burgesses before them and, with these, came to a decision about the representatives. This was done in London, for instance, as early as 1296: "all the aldermen and four citizens from each ward were called together",[3] and on 3 February 1300: "the community was summoned, that is, six of the better and more discreet citizens from each ward".[4]

3. The bailiffs summoned a real borough assembly and the election business was then conducted similarly to that in the county court. This is indicated by expressions such as "they have elected with the assent of the community of the borough"[5] or "the mayor with the assent of the whole community of the borough has elected",[6] and numerous similar phrases. It may be asked in what way these electoral forms are due to differences in the borough constitutions.

---

[1] [Mr Lapsley has suggested to me that Riess has here overlooked two important points: I. That since the county court was normally held in one of the towns that returned members to parliament, the sheriff could have the returns from that town as soon as from the county. II. A phrase in the writs of election of 1295 "ita quod dicti milites plenam et sufficientem potestatem pro se et communitate comitatus praedicti, et dicti cives et burgenses pro se et communitate civitatum et burgorum praedictorum *divisim ab ipsis* tunc ibidem habeant" (Stubbs, *Select Charters*, p. 486) implies that the election of the burgesses was to be made by the boroughs concerned.]

[2] *P.W.* II, ii, 272, 45; 305, 72: "...Ballivi...qui ipsi elegerunt." The relevant words of the quotation p. 272 are "...qui mihi respondent quod... elegerunt...".

[3] *P.W.* I, 49, 41: "...convocati fuerunt omnes Aldermanni ejusdem Civitatis et quatuor homines de singulis wardis ejusdem Civitatis qui omnes unanime assensu et consensu elegerunt...".

[4] *P.W.* I, 85, 8: "convocati fuerunt sex meliores et discretiores cujuslibet wardae pro eligendo duos cives".

[5] *P.W.* I, 73: "quod elegerunt assensu communitatis villae" (Nottingham).

[6] *P.W.* I, 67, 9: "quod elegit assensu communitatis totius villae" (Derby).

But since only a small part of the returns concerning borough elections has been printed; since, moreover, Prynne has made his selection with a conscious bias;[1] since, finally, the constitutional history of the English boroughs in the Middle Ages has not yet been studied, there remains nothing for us but to establish the point that here a gap in our knowledge exists.

[1] Prynne's aim is to give evidence for the widest possible franchise.

CHAPTER IV

The PASSIVE FRANCHISE *from* 1295 *to* 1406

W E MAY now enquire what were the qualifications of those who could be elected, and what rights and duties their parliamentary service involved.

I

Who were eligible as members?

Whereas the Prussian constitutional documents and almost all the other modern constitutions contain only very general and immaterial restrictions with regard to the qualifications of candidates, the mediaeval English law as to elections is, on this point, very strict and exclusive.

Those elected were to be inhabitants of the county which they represented.[1] The writs of election really require this from the first. As early as 1283 the sheriffs were directed "to cause in each county two knights of that county to be elected". Moreover, there can be no doubt that this was observed in practice.

A modification occurs only in so far as many knights were established as landholders in more than one county and so were qualified as candidates for different constituencies. Thus Gerard de Braybroke, who had estates in Buckinghamshire and Bedfordshire, was elected for the former in 1309, and for the latter in 1311; John de la Puyle was, on different occasions, three times a representative of Middlesex, and three times of Surrey. Not until the following period was this freedom restricted.

Those elected are to be important, well-to-do, and vigorous persons. The expressions requiring this are varied in many ways and are, in the nature of the case, vague and elastic.[2]

---

[1] "...quod in quolibet comitatu eligi facerent duos milites...comitatus illius", *R.D.P.* Appendix I, pp. 51, 352, etc. Most of the members can in fact be identified as inhabitants of the counties they represented.

[2] 1283, "de discretioribus et aptioribus". 1290, "de discretioribus et ad laborandum potentioribus". 1299, "de probioribus et legalioribus et discretioribus". 1324, "de melioribus et discretioribus" etc.

But the force of these restrictions, which appear to have reserved the candidature to the highest social orders, must not be over-estimated. For, since in England there were no exclusive classes, it could not constitute a special prerogative of a privileged class.

It was, indeed, obvious that only the well-to-do could be elected, since only such persons were in the position to bear the expenses of the journey and of the stay in the distant place, for which they would not be reimbursed until some time after their return home.

To those who had once been elected, the description *discretiores* could not well be denied, and physical fitness was required because only on vigorous persons could be imposed the hardships of a mediaeval journey and the burdens of official work incidental to membership of parliament.

The rule that the representatives shall be knights is not strictly adhered to, even in the writs themselves.[1] Since, moreover, everyone having twenty pounds of rent (forty pounds after 1366) was obliged to become a knight, or to purchase exemption, less weight is to be attached to this outward form. In fact neither the electors in the counties nor the king in parliament were scrupulous about such formalities.

Thus these restrictions which appear so effective had, in our period, no practical significance. Never was a man who had been returned rejected because his personal qualifications were below the legal requirements.

But of the greatest interest are the prohibitions against the election of certain professional classes.

---

[1] In 13 Edward III the commons pray "que deux Chivalers ceynt des espes de chescun Countie soient esluz..." (*Rot. Parl.* ii, 106, 22). Consequently thereafter appeared in the writs for elections the phrase "milites gladio cinctos"; first in that of 16 November, 13 Edward III (*R.D.P.* Appendix II, p. 508). But already in 47 Edward III "seu armigeros" was inserted, and so the restriction was again raised. This corresponds to a phrase used previously, e.g. in 1299: "milites vel alios".
[The demand for knights girt with swords occurs only intermittently in the writs from 1339 onwards and is probably to be explained by a desire on the part of the central government to secure the election of military men who would be enthusiastic supporters of the war. The same purpose may be seen in the modification of the demand, introduced in 1373, "or esquires more approved by feats of arms" (*R.D.P.* iii, 661). I have discussed the question at length in "Sheriffs, Lawyers, and Belted Knights in the Parliaments of Edward III", *E.H.R.* xlvi, 372–88.]

Especially the sheriffs are not to be elected, "but it is not our will that you or any other sheriff of our kingdom be in any wise elected" regularly occurs in all the writs to the sheriffs from 1373 to 1406.[1] But long before this, as early as 1301, an election was held to replace one of the chosen representatives because he, in the meantime, had been appointed sheriff.[2]

This prohibition is to be explained by the purpose of parliament, described above, to facilitate the control over the sheriffs. In the first generation it was quite obvious that it would be contrary to the interests of the electors themselves, and therefore absurd to send their sheriff to parliament. Not until after certain sheriffs in the years 1320, 1321 and 1322 had, nevertheless, found means of procuring their own election[3] did an express stipulation become necessary.[4]

In like manner, lawyers were made ineligible on account of their profession; "they shall not be advocates or attorneys or persons living by such professions" is inserted in Edward III's writs of election of 1352.[5] The reason for this is given later, when this prohibition is repeated in a statute of 1372; "Because lawyers who pursue divers business in the king's court for private persons whose [attorneys] they are, procure and cause to be accepted in parliament many petitions in the name of the commons, which do not at all concern them but only the private

---

[1] *R.D.P.* Appendix II, 661 ff. The statute on which this formula is based is in *Rot. Parl.* II, 310, 13 and *Statutes of the Realm*, I, 394.

[2] *P.W.* I, 100, 38: "Joh. de Clyntone de Makstoke electus est nunc loco Philippi de Geyton eo quod idem Phil. nunc est Vicecomes Com. Warr. et Leyc...."

[3] These are:

1320.	John Darcy le Cosyn (Nottingham').	*P.W.* II, ii,	226, 23.
	Robert Beudyn (Devon').	,,	222, 11.
	William de Nevill (Leicester').	,,	228, 28.
1321.	Roger de Elmerigg (Hereford').	,,	238, 14.
	Philip de la Beche (Wiltshire).	,,	242, 24.
1322.	Roger de Chaundos (Hereford').	,,	251, 55.
	Walter de Stickeland (Westmorland).	,,	257, 72.
1324.	Adam Walraund (Wiltshire).	,,	310, 83.

[4] [The practice of returning sheriffs to parliament began earlier than Riess supposes, the first sheriff known to have served as a knight of the shire being Miles Pychard, sheriff of Herefordshire from Michaelmas 1300 to April 1303, who represented that county in the parliament which met in October 1302 (*E.H.R.* XLVI, 373).]

[5] *R.D.P.* II, Appendix, 593: "qui non sint placitatores querelarum manutentores aut ex hujusmodi quaestu viventes".

persons by whom they have been engaged [as attorneys]",[1] no lawyers shall henceforth be returned to parliament.

With regard to this class, then, it is improper that they report as advocates the cases of their clients before the highest court, and as guardians of the law recommend those amendments that they, who are in the pay of one party, wish to carry out. Thus they are too little "publicum commodum diligentes", as the above-cited writ of election puts it.[2]

This exception, too, accords well with the duties and purpose of the elected representatives of the country, as these have been explained in Chapter I.

II

The legal consequences of the election with regard to those elected

With us the person elected must first formally declare himself willing to undertake the mandate before the duties and rights of a representative of the country are committed to him, and he can, at any time, by a statement of his wishes, free himself from the obligation, i.e. resign the mandate.

The question is whether in mediaeval England other rules were observed.

The principle appears to be quite clear that the person elected was absolutely bound to go to parliament as the representative of his constituency.

This is shown most clearly by the fact that every man elected was required by the sheriff to find sureties for his appearance at the appointed time and place.[3] With what strictness, moreover, the chancery held to the requirement of punctual attendance is to be seen from a final clause which, after 21 Edward III, often

---

[1] *Rot. Parl.* II, 310, 13: "Purce que Gentz de Ley qui pursuent diverses busoignes en les Courts le Roi pur singulers persones ove queux ils sont, procurent & font mettre plusours Petitions en Parlementz en noñ des Communes, qui rien lour touche mes soulement les singulers persones ove queux ils sont demorez...."   [2] *R.D.P.* II, Appendix, 593.
[3] Usually two sureties sufficed. But when the person elected could not or would not find sureties, he was distrained by his own possessions. E.g. *P.W.* I, 119, 23: "Qui districti sunt per terras et catalla, quia pleg.[iarios] invenire noluerunt"; *P.W.* I, 60, 33: "Ricus de Wyndesore districtus est per catalla ad valenciam x librarum"; *P.W.* I, 66, 5: "Ric. de Rous... districtus est per octo boves et quatuor affros."

recurs in the writs of election: "We intend by no means to excuse or to grant pardon to anyone summoned to the said parliament who is not personally present on the first day."

Moreover, chancery actually took account of this matter. In a surviving list of attendance of 1307[1] a list of those elected has been taken from the sheriffs' returns and a *hic* or a dot placed opposite the names of those who were present, but a cross opposite those who were still absent.[2] Later the rolls of parliament very often mention a roll-call at the beginning of parliament.

The representative was by no means free to resign his mandate. We have already seen that Philip Courtenay had to petition the king "to be released from the said duty" for the time of an impending investigation concerning him. Otherwise those elected must remain present in parliament until the king ended the session and expressly granted them permission to return home.

It already appears then that election constituted an imperative duty for those elected, and the one-sidedness of this conception is shown in a still clearer light from the fact that exemption from election was granted by the king as a special favour to individuals. An exemption of 27 Edward III dispensed James de Audele for life from attendance in parliament and from military service.[3] Richard II even freed a man, who had been already elected, "from the office of knight in the said parliament" and required the election of another.[4] The young king also granted the same favour to Thomas Morwell, a vassal of his mother.[5] But that

---

[1] Printed in *P.W.* I, 183 ff.

[2] In this manner forty-nine out of 248 representatives are designated as absent, namely, eight knights of the shire (one from each of eight counties) and forty-one representatives of boroughs (two from each of eighteen towns and one from each of five). Only for Peter de Salso, knight, of Worcestershire is an excuse given (*P.W.* I, 187).

[3] Rymer, *Foedera*, H. III, pars I, p. 84. [James de Audele was a baron personally summoned to parliament, not a knight liable to election.]

[4] *R.D.P.* Appendix I, pt. II, 707: "Nos advertentes, quod...ipsum de officio militis ad dictum parliamentum...venturi exonerare volumus." [The man who was thus freed from attendance was Thomas Camoys; he is described as a banneret and the exemption was granted on the ground that bannerets were not wont to serve as knights of the shire. These criticisms, however, do not disprove Riess's theory in support of which genuine cases of exemptions from parliamentary service granted to men whose social position rendered them liable to election as knights of the shire might be cited; e.g. that issued in favour of Bernard Brocas in 1381 (*Cal. Pat. Rolls*, 1381–5, p. 26).]

[5] *R.D.P.* Appendix I, pt. II, 707.

such express exemptions were possible and necessary is the best proof of the strength of the rule.[1]

III

The personal rights of the representatives

All previous investigators, especially Hallam,[2] Cox, Stubbs,[3] Gneist,[4] Taswell-Langmead,[5] concur in the belief that "from the beginning, the commons claimed freedom of speech in Parliament as a matter of course" and with a few exceptions "always enjoyed the privilege of not being held responsible for their motions and debates".

The contrary of this opinion can be proved to be correct, for the following reasons:

1. Nowhere, during our whole period, is there to be found any indication of the granting of such a privilege to the commons, of its being claimed by the lower house, or even of an appeal to such a right. Indeed, although it is the custom for the speaker

---

[1] Palgrave, in the Introduction to his *Parliamentary Writs*, refers to two returns in which are named representatives other than those who afterwards received their writs *de expensis* where no explanation can be given (Preface, vi). Now these two cases can easily be seen to be mere errors. In the writs *de expensis* (*P.W.* II, ii, 325, 39), instead of the two knights mentioned in the return (*ibid.* 319, 12), the names of the manucaptors have been casually copied:

[Manucaptor] Robtus Clement Thomas Clement ⎫ In Writs *de expensis*
[„] Joħes de Loundř Joħes [de] Bundre ⎭ *P.W.* II, ii, 325, 39.
P.W. II, ii, 68, 67. Instead of the names from the return (60, 45) the representatives in the previous parliament (46, 6) have been erroneously copied from the chancery certificate which was serving as a model. But for four other cases which appear in the Calendar, I have not been able to find the source of the errors. I assume, however, that one certainly exists, since there can be no thought of substitution.

[2] *Constitutional History*, p. 68: "No privilege of the commons can be so fundamental as liberty of speech."

[3] *Constitutional History*, III, 489 ff.

[4] *Englische Verfassungsgeschichte*, p. 383.

[5] *Constitutional History*, 2nd ed. p. 320: "Freedom of speech, the essential attribute of every free legislature, may be regarded as inherent in the constitution of Parliament." This is indeed only a misrepresentation and adaptation of a philosophical reflection of May in an historical sketch; Cf. May, *Parliamentary Practice* (4th ed. 1859), p. 108: "Freedom of speech is a privilege essential to every free council or legislature. It is so necessary... that if it had never been expressly confirmed, it must still have been acknowledged as inseparable from Parliament, and inherent in its constitution." May, of course, had in mind only the parliament of to-day, whose legal position he wished to set forth.

of the lower house to ask for himself and receive special consideration, nothing at all is said of any freedom of speech of the body which he had to represent. We must reflect, moreover, that such a special prayer of the speaker for himself would have been altogether unnecessary if every member of parliament had really enjoyed full liberty of speech, for the speaker was himself a member.[1]

2. Furthermore, it can be definitely proved that there were cases in which representatives were punished and thrown into prison on account of their candid speech. Henry de Keighly, a representative of Lancashire, was, in 1301, the first of the series,[2] and neither he nor his later fellow-sufferers appealed to their immunity from being held responsible; no more did the house require the liberation of its members. On one occasion, even the whole lower house did not escape without humiliation on account of its boldness. When the commons in 1397 introduced complaints about the squandering of money on the bishops whom the king had about him, and on the ladies who lived at his expense, Richard II became furious and demanded from whom the commons had received information as to the amount of these expenses. He punished the man who had supplied abstracts of the accounts, and the representatives begged and received pardon.[3]

No better proof could be found for the fact that during our period the members enjoyed no freedom of speech than these examples of successful punishment which Stubbs himself enumerates. If Stubbs will, nevertheless, hold to his opinion, he must prove these cases which contradict his view to have been exceptions, that is, he must produce evidence that in numerous other instances equally bold or bolder speeches were made, or unwelcome motions were introduced; that the king had wished to inflict punishment, but had not been able to do so on account of the privileges of the representatives. But Stubbs has made not the least attempt to do this.[4]

[1] The substance of the speakers' petitions is given by Stubbs, *Constitutional History*, III, 454.
[2] *Ibid.* II, 151. The list of further cases is described in detail by Stubbs, III, 490 ff.   [3] *Rot. Parl.* III, 339, 16.
[4] *Constitutional History*, III, 490. He suggests that this privilege was established more "by results than by details". But this can by no means be

The other English scholars proceed in a different way. They pass over all other cases in silence and stop at only one incident, which concerns Thomas Haxey and which seems to them to have especially conclusive force. Thomas Haxey was the bearer of the abstracts of accounts, whose punishment has been mentioned above, but the fact that he was not a member of the lower house, but a chancery official, deprives this precedent of its conclusiveness.[1] Moreover, his pardon was prayed for not by the commons, but by the archbishops, and was brought about through his status as a clerk; he was released from custody and lost only his position and fortune.[2] Then when Richard had been deposed and his adversary raised to the throne, Haxey, in the first year of Henry IV, sent a petition to parliament for complete restitution to his former financial position.[3] Dissatisfied with the answer, he repeated his request, and added that his punishment had been carried out "encontre droit et la curse quel avoit este devaunt en Parlement".[4] But this assertion made by one who was so personally interested, who aimed at winning a legal claim thereby, cannot in the least prove the freedom of speech of the representatives. Moreover, Haxey was not able to derive any advantage for himself from this right, since his petition remained unanswered.

Thus there remains only a petition of the commons from the year 1541 wherein among "their old and undoubted rights and privileges" they claim "freedom of speech in all their

admitted. For since it must naturally have been only a rare occurrence that one of the commons "de vos povres Communes", as they style themselves, offended the king, the number of such cases must necessarily have been reduced to a minimum through the mere possibility of a punishment. Consequently the few cases of punishment inflicted are a very strong argument, whereas, of course, nothing can be made of the vast number of cases in which the representatives had not given offence in their speech, since these are no proofs of immunity.

[1] On this point, May, *Parliamentary Practice* (4th ed.), p. 109, is in error. [In regarding Haxey as a chancery official, Riess came nearer to the truth than most of the other scholars, who described him as a member of the commons or as a proctor of the lower clergy attending parliament under the *praemunientes* clause. His position was not satisfactorily explained until Tout's *Chapters in Administrative History*, vol. IV, was published in 1928. There (pp. 17–19) it is shown that he was clerk of the Common Bench. Tout further suggests that the king's severity was due to anger at Haxey's desertion of his cause.]

[2] *Rot. Parl.* III, 341, 23.   [3] *Rot. Parl.* III, 430, 90.

[4] *Rot. Parl.* III, 434, 104.

debates".[1] But it is a too frequent and ordinary occurrence in history, that persons endeavouring at favourable opportunities to arrogate to themselves new rights describe these as "ancient rights" which they have long enjoyed for us to be led astray here where the facts are to the contrary.[2]

But also with regard to criminal cases, outside of their parliamentary activities, the members of parliament of our own times are, within certain limits, protected from examination and arrest during a session. This right the English scholars also claim for the members of the Plantagenet period.[3]

Since, however, the parliaments of the Middle Ages had only one session, which was usually very brief; since, further, no one, concerning whom a criminal process was pending, was ever elected; and, finally, since the private conduct of the members outside of parliament never gave the occasion for criminal proceedings, it is hardly possible to say anything positive on this point. But we can by no means agree with Stubbs in deducing from the doubled Wergeld, which was exacted when a member of the Witanagemote was killed or robbed on the way, a protection for criminous members against the higher legal authorities.

On the other hand, it may well be asserted that the idea on which the freedom from arrest of modern members depends, the exceptional importance attached to parliamentary duties, was not yet prevalent.

When those elected for Westmorland cannot come to parliament because they, like all the men between the ages of fifteen and sixty, must, under penalty, appear before a commission of array at the bridge of Amot;[4] when, in Northamptonshire, a new election is ordered because the man elected is occupied with the assessment of taxes in the neighbouring county of Warwick,[5]

---

[1] Printed by Stubbs, *Constitutional History*, III, 455, n. 1. [This does not come from a Commons' petition of 1541, but is found in the Speaker's protestation from 6 Henry VIII onwards.]

[2] In another context Gneist also emphasizes "the usual antedating of the claims of the estates" on the part of the commons (*Englische Verfassungsgeschichte*, p. 374).

[3] Especially Hallam, *Constitutional History*, p. 67; May, *Parliamentary Practice* (4th ed.), p. 117.   [4] *P.W.* I, 44, 31.

[5] The writ which ordered the new election is printed *R.D.P.* Appendix, pp. 120f.

the ordinary course of law would not be disturbed because a person against whom it was directed had become a member of parliament.[1]

The daily expenses of the members were reckoned for every day from the beginning to the end of the parliament and for the time of the journey to and from. That the right to these might be resigned is proved by the lists of those who obtained writs *de expensis* from the chancery, from which the names of individual members of different counties are very often absent. We have already met with the complaint of the county of Lancashire, which had to pay the full sum (four shillings a day) to the members who had been arbitrarily appointed by the sheriff, whereas former members had always been content with half that amount.

Thus we see that the expenses were not paid by the national treasury, but were raised by special assessments on the constituencies[2] and delivered by the sheriff to the representatives who had served. Only against the community concerned had the representative a claim, the state did not assist.

SUMMARY

If now we again examine the structure of the new corporate body, the extremely close connexion of the whole institution with the separate life of the administrative districts is especially striking. The control of the local administration is a principal object of the new creation, which must even furnish the means for the actual administration of certain local affairs.

The summoning of the majority of the constituencies, the boroughs, was not issued directly, but was adapted to the general administrative arrangements.

The election of the county representatives took place in an assembly in which the affairs of the community were to be managed. Those elected should belong to the administrative

---

[1] [The fullest recent account of these matters is given by Mr Jolliffe (*Constitutional History*, pp. 451–5). With regard to freedom of speech during the Lancastrian period he concludes that "though when the issue was raised formally, the commons did not venture to claim complete freedom as to the matter of their petitions, or as to the terms in which they discussed them...a very considerable latitude was accorded in practice". He shows, moreover, that as early as 1314, members enjoyed some measure of freedom from arrest.]   [2] See Appendix I.

district which they represented. They received their expenses from their constituencies.

On the other hand, how little is the common public interest emphasized in them! In the highest decisions of the state they have no certain share. The amount of the taxes was not granted by all the representatives for the whole kingdom, but by the knights for the counties and by the burgesses for the boroughs. Where the slightest claim of the state on any man who had been elected appeared, his mandate would be set aside as of merely provincial interest.

How very different is this elected chamber from the modern one with its far-reaching authority for the whole state and with the responsibilities of its members with regard to national policy!

But how fundamentally does it also differ from the mediaeval assemblies of estates on the Continent with their aspirations based only on privileges and immunities! Moreover, in its internal structure based on the administrative system of the country, the English lower house appears in contrast to the composition of the German Reichstag of the Middle Ages, depending as that did on territorial power or the class interests of groups.

CHAPTER V

The CAUSES *of* MODIFICATION

"The sea is tranquil, reflecting the heavens, then a storm suddenly arises; but when the storm is over the sea is the same. When movement and tempest arise in the life of men, it will likewise again be calm; but meanwhile the world has been altered." *(Works of Ranke, xxxiii, 20.)*

NOT until the institution of the lower house had become an object of international interest did people take the trouble to trace historically its origin and beginnings. Only after the Frenchman, Montesquieu, had published his account of the English parliamentary system and the whole of educated Europe had been carried away with admiration for the political freedom of Great Britain, did the English upper house arrange for the publication of the ancient parliamentary writs, and Blackstone undertake his comprehensive "Commentaries" which even to-day still enjoy, in England, classical authority.

Thus it is not surprising that the first authors of the early Parliamentary History were led by their preconceptions to express views and hypotheses which cannot be accepted without question.

In full possession of political freedom and in the blaze of the general admiration, the English could not think otherwise than that the rights which they enjoyed had been rights at all times, that their ancestors could always share in the privileges which seemed to belong as an inheritance to the English alone among the civilized peoples. It was precisely this idea of the indubitable originality of the parliamentary form of constitution which created in them the desire to set forth the glory of the English commonwealth, even in the distant past.

This point of view has been retained more or less by all the English scholars until to-day [1885]. All of them assume that the fundamental characteristics of the modern English constitution were already present in the earliest times; that they always retained their value; that, after temporary obscurity, they again came forth in their old force; and that in the consciousness of successive generations they were increasingly understood and prized. These men feel that they have done enough for the requirements of historical understanding when in the extant material they point out the oldest, clearest and most significant cases of precedent which are in accord with their previously formed opinion.

But let us not conceal from ourselves that with this interpretation—which shows in the centuries of history only a revival of tradition, a finding of more secure forms which are better suited to the times—any investigation into the antiquities of the English parliament would lose for us its real interest. Thus the attempt to trace historically and to understand the genesis of the lower house, which was one day to furnish the model for European constitutions, would have to be abandoned; just as we cannot approach historically nearer to another institution, which, however, is immemorial, the origin of kingship.

Through Gneist's epoch-making researches, however, it has been fully demonstrated how completely continuity was broken by the Norman Conquest, and a new social order, involving new administrative arrangements, put in the place of the Anglo-Saxon commonwealth. The various stages of this new form of government were first treated in detail and made clear by German scholars. There can no longer be any doubt that, except in the case of the organization of the Judiciary, all that developed later must have had its origin in the historically known period after the time of William the Conqueror.[1]

In particular, we have traced the creation of the lower house and the electoral law during the first period entirely to the conditions of the thirteenth century and to the purpose of Edward I. As yet the Commons had no common rights, and no corporate duties: the right of granting taxes had not been conceded to them, legislation was not dependent on their assent,[2] a directing influence over the central government was entirely outside the sphere of their activities. No wonder that the elections to such a national assembly attracted little attention.

---

[1] Cf. the essay by Noorden, "Zur Geschichte und Literatur des englischen Selfgovernment", *Historische Zeitschrift*, XIII, 23 ff.
[2] See Appendix III.

Now, under the Lancastrian kings the parliamentary suffrage, as has already been said, has become the subject of detailed regulations, county elections have become the battle-ground of political parties and the cause of intense excitement.

[Here follows a long discussion of economic history which, as I have explained in the introduction, it has not seemed desirable to retain.]

CHAPTER VI

SURVEY *of the* ATTEMPTS *at* REFORM, 1406–1461

IN THE parliament of 1406, the two houses jointly laid before the king thirty-one articles, to all of which he assented. One of these prescribed, with regard to the elections, that in all the market towns of each county, proclamation of the day and place of the county court should be made fourteen days in advance, in order that the sufficient persons of the county might attend.[1]

It is noteworthy that another of these articles states that all the regulations which they contain are to remain in force only until the end of the next parliament. From this it is apparent how little the two allied houses were united in their efforts, and so it is not surprising that in the very next parliament Henry IV obtained the commons' assent to the annulment of this statute, and thus the upper house was to some extent outvoted.

But in that same parliament of 1406 the commons made a special demand with regard to the elections which became law and remained permanently in force. The question is what relation did this bear to the joint plan just mentioned.

Let us consider the situation. On account of the commons' bold demands, especially that for the answering of petitions before money grants were made, the relations between the king and the lower house had reached the breaking point. This moment the lords used to ally themselves with the other house and, with the help of the commons, to force on the king their most far-reaching demands and make them law. In order permanently to assure to themselves a lower house in which they would have influence, they required a special arrangement by which precisely those classes which habitually absented themselves from the

---

[1] *Rot. Parl.* III, 588, 83: "...Qe proclamation soit faite en toutes les Villes Marches du Countee du Jour & Lieu ou les ditz Chivalers serront esluz xv jour devaunt le jour d'Election; aufin q̃ les suffisantz persones enhabitantz en le dit Countee y puissent estre, pur faire Election...."

county court should be informed in good time of the day and
place of an election, so that by the veto of their dependents, who
would flock to the election, the choice of undesirable knights
could at any time be prevented.

Rather than risk more objectionable legislation concerted by
the king and the upper house, the isolated lower house concurred in this. But while they limited the duration of the new
law to one year only, they at the same time had it in mind to
protect themselves permanently against the worst use of force
in the elections. By conceding that those who had only come on
account of the election should share in the choice of members,
they obtained the assent of the lords to the three following
points: First, that an open election in the county court should be
definitely assured. It was provided that at the next county
court after the summoning of a parliament, the day and place of
the parliament should be made known by a proclamation.[1] Then
all who were present in the assembly should proceed at once to
the election without being influenced in any way either by en-
treaties or commands.[2] Finally, in order to guard against false
returns for the future, the return, with the names of those
elected even when these were absent, was to be drawn up in the
form of an indenture and sealed by all the electors.[3] The writs
of summons, from now on, contain quite definite instructions
to that effect,[4] and instead of the old returns there follow indentures with seals attached.

In the *Paston Letters* there are concrete examples showing how
much importance the lords attached to having their dependents
elected as members, and how they sought to achieve this end
through the participation of their followers in the elections.

---

[1] *Rot. Parl.* III, 601, 139: "...C'est assavoir, qe al prochein Counte a
tenir apres la liveree du Brief du Parlement, proclamation soit fait en plein
Countee de la Jour & Lieu de Parlement."
[2] *Ibid.*: "Et qe toutz ceux qi illeoqes sont presents, si bien sueters duement
sommonez p. cell cause, come autres, attendent le Election de lour Chivalers
pur le Parlement; & adonqes en plein Countee aillent a l'Election, liberalment,
& indifferentement, non-obstant ascun prier ou commandement du contraire."
[3] *Ibid.*: "Et apres q'ils soient esluz, soient les persones esluz presentz ou
absentz, soient lour Nouns escriptz en Endenture dessoutz les Sealx de toutz
ceux qi eux eslisent, & tacchez au dit Brief du Parlement. Quele Endenture
issint ensealez & tacchez soit tenuz pur Retourne du dit Brief quaunt as
Chivalers des Countees."
[4] *R.D.P.* II, Appendix, 802,f. (8 Henry IV).

One might, however, hesitate to draw from these events, which
took place during the civil war, conclusions as to the period
before the outbreak of the Wars of the Roses.[1] But it is emi-
nently noteworthy how the lower house and the king took increasingly effective measures against the influences from without,
how they endeavoured to reserve the parliamentary elections
ever more surely to that class of the population which had
dominated them in the preceding period, which was alone independent of the barons, and which, moreover, felt itself to be,
to some extent, in opposition to the latter.

In the year 1413 the commons demanded and the king assented
to an additional clause in the statute of elections requiring that
those elected as well as the electors must, at the time, belong to
the counties whose representation was concerned.[2] The first
of these requirements had always been commanded by the
wording of the writs, the other had been taken for granted; but
now that the elections had gained importance, legal recognition
was necessary. In such legislative acts which protected the
existing legal position, it is especially important to see what was
really to be guarded against. The commons say in their petition
that "the election shall not be made by the votes, nor by the
consent, nor by the command of those who are absent".[3]
In this we see the great barons behind the scenes of the
election affecting the decisions through their followers and
their influence.

Especially through the restriction of eligibility it was believed
that a lower house, independent of the barons, could be assured.
A statute of 1445 laid it down "that the representatives of the
counties in parliament shall be notable knights of the same
counties for which they shall be elected, or otherwise such
notable esquires, and gentlemen by birth, of the same counties
as are capable of becoming knights; and no man who is of the

[1] *Paston Letters*, I, 63, 111, 173; II, 56, 70.
[2] *Rot. Parl.* IV, 8, 20: "Adjoustantz a ycelles, qe les Chivalers esluz pur
Parlement soient receantz & demurrantz a temps de l'Election es Countes ou
ils sont esluz: Et qe mesmes les Chivalers soient esluz p Chivalers, Esquiers,
& Communes des Countes ou ils sont issint esluz, & nemy en autre manere...."
To the same effect is *Statutes of the Realm*, II, 170, i (1413), so also the re-
inforcement of this, *ibid.* 235, iv (1427).
[3] *Ibid.*: "...& nemye p voice, ne l'assent, ne maundement, de ceux q̃ sont
absentz".

rank of yeoman or lower shall be a member".[1] To this were added numerous threats of punishment for the sheriffs and bailiffs whose procedure in holding the elections was incorrect; they must pay a fine of a hundred pounds to the king and the defrauded party.

All these stipulations, however, do not really indicate a growth of the electoral procedure; even in the previous period they had been at least practically in force, or at any rate implied.

On the other hand, the newly awakened political life showed itself with regard to the forms of elections to be creative in two respects. A statute of 1429 states also the motives which had led to its framing. There it is said, "since the elections of the knights of the shire in many counties of England...have been carried out by a great and excessive number of persons (who dwell in the same counties) of whom the greater number are persons of small substance or of no consequence, and since everyone of these claims to have, in such elections, an equal voice with the best knights and esquires who dwell in the same counties, and since, consequently, homicides, riots, assaults and divisions between the gentlemen and the other people will probably arise and take place if no suitable remedy is provided".[2]

Here, for the first time, emerges the idea that participation in the election was a political right, and one which did not belong unquestionably to every inhabitant of the constituency, still less to all in the same degree.

In a quite primitive manner it was settled that all inhabitants of the county who did not possess freehold land to the value of

[1] *Statutes of the Realm*, II, 342, ff., xiv: "Issint que les Chivalers dez Counteez pur le Parlement en apres a esliers soient notablez Chivalers dez mesmez lez Counteez pur les queux ils serront issint esluz, ou autrement tielx notablez Esquiers gentils homez del [Nativite] dez mesmez les Counteez come soient ablez destre Chivalers; & null home destre tiel Chivaler que estoise en la degree de vadlet & dessouth."

[2] *Statutes of the Realm*, II, 243, vii: "Item come lez eleccions dez Chivalers des Countees esluz a venir as parlements du Roi en plusours Countees Dengleterre, ore tarde ounte este faitz par trop graunde & excessive nombre dez gentz demurrantz deinz mesmes les Countes, dount la greindre partie estoit par gentz sinon de petit avoir ou de null valu, dount chescun pretende davoire [voice] equivalent quant a tielx eleccions faire ove les pluis valantz chivalers ou esquiers demurrantz deins mesmes les Countees; dount homicides riotes batteries & devisions entre les gentiles & autres gentz des mesmes les Countees verisemblablement sourdront & serront, si covenable remedie ne soit purveu en celle partie."

forty shillings a year were excluded from the right, and all who possessed more should have an equal share.[1] What is most important, the first step towards the constitution of an electoral assembly was not omitted; the sheriffs were fully empowered to cause everyone taking part in the elections to swear on the Gospels that he possessed the required annual income.[2]

The other development appears at once. In this statute the idea of the majority is conceived for the first time when it is laid down that the greater number shall take the place of the whole.[3] All the writs of election from the time of Henry VI repeat that those men shall be held to be elected "qui habuerint majorem numerum ipsorum, qui quadraginta solidos per annum & ultra expendere possunt...".[4]

Nowhere else, as far as I know, had the absolute right of the majority found legal expression in the Middle Ages. It is known how the German Electors, in spite of the most obstinate struggles during the elections, always held to the formal procedure of voting unanimously; and how long the Cardinals often waited in Conclave on account of the required unanimity. Where a community and an individual had to act together as in the case of the election of bishops, the royal commissioner shall, when the chapter is divided, hold to the "sanior pars"; there is no talk of a majority. Even the mediaeval judge shall decide "by command and direction of the more prudent of the twelve".[5] What a

---

[1] *Statutes of the Realm*, II, 243, vii: "...que les Chivalers des Countes... soient esluz en chescun Counte par gentz demurrantz & receantz en icelles, dount chescun ait frank tenement a le valu de xl. s. par an al meins outre les reprises;...Purveu toutfoitz que celluy qi ne poet expendre xl. s. p. an,...ne soit en ascun manere eslisour des Chivalers pur le parlement."

[2] *Statutes of the Realm*, II, 243, vii: "Et ait chescun Vicont Dengleterre poair par auctorite suisdite dexaminer sur les seintz Evangelies chescun tiel eslisour, comebien il poet expendre par an:...."

[3] *Statutes of the Realm*, II, 243, vii: "...& ceux qui ount le greindre nombre de yceulx qi poient expendre p. an xl.s. & outre...soient retournez... Chivalers pur le parlement...."

[4] *Report on the Dignity of a Peer*, II, Appendix, 877.

[5] Britton, *Treatise of Law*, I, 23. [This passage, taken from the section "of Eyres of Justices", concerns the compilation of the record of present-ments and has nothing to do with the decision of law suits: "He (the justice) shall then read the articles distinctly in English. And that which they shall present he shall put first in a roll, which shall be their note and shall remain with them. And afterwards of that and the other things, by command and direction of the more prudent of the twelve, he shall make his chief roll." With regard to the verdict of the jury, Britton, unlike other mediaeval

complicated procedure the *Modus tenendi Parliamentum* pre-
scribes for the case in which all, or at least the great majority,
are not of the same opinion; here twenty-five shall first be
chosen, and if these cannot agree, they shall choose twelve
from among themselves, and these, in case of dissension, shall
choose six; these, in like case, may choose three; finally the
number may come down to two, whose unanimous decision
shall be binding on all.[1] Now, through experience of existing
election contests in all parts of the kingdom, entirely different
ideas had been evolved.

The way in which the majority was now determined, as well
as the further questions that here arise, I am not able to discuss
because from the almost complete series of later election returns
that are now kept in the national archives in London, nothing
more has been printed since Prynne's publication of 1664.

But there is no doubt that from the incomparably comprehensive documentary material contained in the Public Record
Office, and with the aid of the pamphlets and collections of
letters in the British Museum, most valuable studies could be
made of the history of elections to the English parliament and,
therewith, of English political life.

Perhaps it will one day be possible for me to continue the
work begun here down to the far-reaching attempts at reform
of our own century.

jurists, seems to recognize the majority principle: "If they cannot all agree
in one mind, let them be separated and examined why they cannot agree;
and if the greater part of them know the truth and the other part do not,
judgment shall be according to the opinion of the greater part" (I, 31, 10).]
[1] "De cassibus et judiciis difficilibus": a remarkable special chapter of
the *Modus tenendi Parliamentum*. See Appendix IV.

APPENDIX I (TO CHAPTER III)

The DUTY *of* CONTRIBUTING *to the* KNIGHTS' WAGES, 1295–1406

It is by no means to be assumed *a priori* that only those who were represented paid the expenses, and that only those who took part, or could take part, in the elections were represented.[1]

But when, as happened in our period, the duty of contributing was contested, some light at least is thrown on the existing relations between election and representation, and on contemporary opinion concerning them.

Here it is most striking that in all cases where a definitive regulation of the disputed conditions is sought, the answer of the king which follows is "let the ancient custom be observed".[2]

From this we may probably conclude: 1, that the conditions of payment were based on tradition, and were different in different counties, for which reason any general ruling had to allow for wide exceptions; 2, that the rules of participation in elections and the idea of being represented were not definitely settled, and were not sufficiently regarded to be depended upon for any shire. For the connexion between these three concepts could not and, as we shall see, did not pass unobserved.

But if we examine in detail the development of the obligation to contribute, that is to say, of the efforts to interfere with it, we shall gain a new means of testing our positive account of the laws of elections in the following respects:

1. It was to the interest of the knights of the shire that the duty of contributing to their expenses should be extended as far as possible. The limits to which their desires reached must, however, appear as the natural consequence of the conditions of the elections which we have assumed above; but they would have to set forth the most extreme possibilities that were in their favour.

---

[1] Cox, *Antient Parliamentary Elections*, p. 88 and Stubbs, *Constitutional History*, II, 224f., 231, are in error on this point.

[2] So in the years 1354 (*Rot. Parl.* II, 258, 23): "Soit fait come ad este faite avant ces heures"; 1364 (*Rot. Parl.* II, 287, 20): "Soit fait come ad este fait & usee avant ces heurs"; 1376 (*Rot. Parl.* II, 368, 45): "Soit fait come devant ad este use en ce cas"; 1378 (*Rot. Parl.* III, 44, 57): "Ent soit fait come ad este use devant ces heures"; 1378 (*Rot. Parl.* III, 53, 10): "Soit use come avant ces heures ad este"; 1385 (*Rot. Parl.* III, 212, 24): "Soit come ad este usez devant ces heurs"; 1388 (*St. R.* II, 59, xii): "Soit faite come ad este use avant ces hures"; 1391 (*Rot. Parl.* III, 293, 37): "Soit use come ad este use devaunt ces heures".

2. It will have to be explained that the proportion of contributions remained far below this extreme computation.

3. It will appear why the king could not regard the wish of the petitioning commons as suited to the real conditions, and why, between the insufficient reality and these claims, a middle course could not be found that would appear rational, satisfactory and just.

Originally it was probably taken for granted that all the inhabitants of the county should contribute to the expenses as to other taxes. Through arbitrary interference on the part of the king, doubts and confusion as to the conditions of contribution first arose. In 1307 Edward I commanded that the tenants of John de la Mare should not be charged because he had been personally summoned and had attended.[1] In 1322 the villeins of the bishop of Norwich were similarly exempted.[2]

But when the king, at the request of individual barons who were personally summoned, thus exempted their tenants from the obligation of contributing to the expenses, a precedent was created which all who felt themselves to be in the same position could make use of, and to which many had recourse.

In order to avert this consequence which was felt to be unjust, the commons, in 1354, begged for a declaration as to whether such exemptions should be valid or not.[3] To this the king gave the noteworthy answer "let the ancient custom be observed"; that is, he avoided any definite ruling. The reason for this is, of course, that he could not assent to one extreme, the complete freeing of all the tenants of the lords, and that the other extreme was incompatible with previous grants of exemption. Ten years later the commons renewed their petition, but again without success.[4]

One can imagine how this lack of regulation made itself felt in the actual levying of the expenses. Those who had once been freed probably held to their privilege even when their lord was no longer summoned. Other magnates claimed for their peasants the same privilege as the barons who were summoned; one case of this kind has come down to us.[5]

[1] *P.W.* I, 191, 16. Also printed by Cox, *Antient Parliamentary Elections*, p. 89. [2] *P.W.* II, ii, 259, 77.
[3] *Rot. Parl.* II, 258, 23: "...come les tenantz les Seigneurs qi tiegnent par Baronie & sont somons au Parlement, claiment estre deschargez de les despenses des Chivalers...". [4] *Rot. Parl.* II, 287, 20.
[5] Rymer, *Foedera*, H. III, pars III, p. 54 (16 January 1377): "Rex vicecomiti Bed' salutem. Cum Communitates cujuslibet comitatus Regni nostri...ad Expensas Militum, ad Parliamentum, pro Communitate Comitatus praedicti, venientium, contribuere debeant,...Ac jam intelleximus quod Egidius Daubeneye et Fulco de Pembrugge, Domini Manerii de Kempton,...Praetendentes, Se et Tenentes suos, Liberos et Nativos Manerii praedicti, de contributione...expensarum quietos esse debere... contradicunt....Nos attendentes quod omnes Domini Maneriorum et

In the face of these conditions which were changing for the worse the commons adopted new tactics for bringing about a reasonable arrangement. They now sought to justify their claims and to make them acceptable to the king. Since the members represented the community of the counties, apart from the prelates, dukes, earls, barons and others who were personally summoned (if the towns which were represented are excluded), all the commons of the counties, except the burgesses and those who were personally summoned and their villeins, should contribute towards the expenses.[1] In still more definite terms the commons demanded from Richard II "...that everyone of whatever rank he might be, within liberties as well as without, and from whomsoever he held his land should be bound to contribute towards the expenses of the said members; as right and reason require, except the lords who come to parliament by special summons and remain there at their own cost, and their villeins".[2]

These demands of the commons are an entirely logical consequence of the conditions of participation in the elections as we have described them; at the same time some allowance was made for the customary exemptions. That the king did not agree to this is due in the first place to the great divergency between what was desired and what existed in the different counties. Moreover, it was perhaps equally justified to limit the duty of contributing to those who, on account of their position in the county court, could if they wished offer effective opposition.

This view was in fact held, as appears from two petitions. In 1378 the representatives of Kent pray "...that the members for the county of Kent shall receive their expenses from the commons of the said county in the same way as other knights of the shire in the kingdom are paid, although the said payments were formerly raised from the fees of the knights of the said county".[3]

Their reason for wishing to alter the custom is interesting. For it is based not on the conditions of participation in the elections but on the expected rise in the amount of the wages as a consequence of the increasing frequency of parliaments. No wonder that the king would not grant their request.[4]

Villarum, qui Barones non existunt, et qui ad Parliamentum nostrum, de Mandato nostro, non veniunt, nec de jure venire consueverint, ac omnes libere Tenentes et Nativi sui, hujusmodi Expensis de Jure contribuere debeant,..." the sheriff shall compel them to pay.

[1] *Rot. Parl.* II, 368, 45.
[2] *Rot. Parl.* III, 212, 24.   [3] *Rot. Parl.* III, 53, 10.
[4] *Rot. Parl.* III, 53, 10: "...Eaunt regard, q̃ en temps a vener est ordeigne de tener plusours Parlements qui n'ount este devant ces houres, a tres grant charge as tenants de dits fees, s'ils ne eient eide en manere suisdit." [Miss L. C. Latham, who has made the fullest study of the collection of the knights'

Finally the commons, in 1391, demanded that all the lords of manors within liberties should contribute towards the expenses. Even on this point the king issued no regulation that should be generally binding, but only ordered that they should complain of individual cases.[1]

The only statute of our period that deals with the incidence of these levies likewise lays it down that "the old custom shall be observed", and is only concerned that the estates which, according to custom, were bound to contribute, should not escape this liability if they should come into the hands of a baron.[2]

When all these are taken together it can be said:

1. That in a number of counties, during a period of unobserved natural development, the position had been reached that all the inhabitants of the county (with the exception of numerous individuals privileged for special reasons) had to contribute towards the wages of the representatives. Here the first mentioned principle, that all who had the right of attending and assenting to elections should contribute, was, on the whole, recognized.

2. In Kent, and probably in a considerable number of other counties, only the more important people, the lords of manors, paid. There the second principle was in force; he who could definitely influence the elections by his veto contributed to the expenses.

3. The principal exception arose from the fact that the dependants of those who were personally summoned were exempted by the king from contributing, although they remained free to take part in the

---

wages that has so far appeared, writes: "Tenants in Kentish gavelkind were also an exempt class, a fact which explains the special difficulties that seem to have been attached to the recovery of their wages by the Kentish knights. Kentish contributors were of course in a particularly disadvantageous position, owing to the absence of villeinage and the exemption of gavelkind lands, which latter represented some two-thirds of the shire. Contribution was then an incident that attached exclusively to tenure by knight service and to a strictly limited number of such tenements and it was in vain that the county in 1378 petitioned that its representatives 'soient paies de lour gages par les communes du dit counte, en maniere come autres chivalers sont paies...non obstante qe les ditz gages devant ses heures ount este levez par les fees de chivaler du dit counte'" (*E.H.R.* XLVIII, 458, 461).]

[1] *Rot. Parl.* III, 293, 37.

[2] *Statutes of the Realm*, II, 59, xii (12 Richard II): "Item, endroit de la levee des despences des Chivalers venantz as parlementz pur les communes des Countees, accordez est & assentuz, qe la dicte levee soit faite come ad este use avant ces hures; ajouste a ycelle q̃ si ascun seigneur ou autre homme espirituel ou temporel eit purchacez ascuns terres ou tenementz ou outres possessions qi soleient estre contributoires as tiels despences devant le temps du dit purchase, q̃ mesmes les terres tenementz & possessions & les tenants dicelles soient contributoirs as dites despenses come les ditz terres tenementz & possessions et les tenantz dicelles soleient faire devant le temps de mesme la purchace."

election. The real struggle was over this point. The question was whether all the tenants of those who were summoned, the freeholders and knights—not merely the villeins—who lived within their liberties should be excused.

4. The king could not decide for a uniform system according to this or that rule, nor could he hold to a middle course, without annulling the grants made by his ancestors which had resulted in the conditions just described and destroying the customary privileges of those who were personally summoned.

He did what, on the whole, was most conformable to the circumstances, when he legalized, now one arrangement, now another, with regard to the duty of payment—the exemptions that were based on tradition, and those depending on them that had crept in—by his invariable "let the ancient custom be observed".

APPENDIX II (TO CHAPTER IV)

The APPOINTMENT *of* SURETIES *for the*
BOROUGH REPRESENTATIVES

The question is whether the appointment of the sureties for the representatives of the towns was managed by the sheriff as the election commissioner who was directly responsible, or whether it fell to the bailiffs who conducted the election in the borough.

As our material says little positively, the answer can only be found in an indirect way.

Normally knights and burgesses had two sureties each; but now and then—quite sporadically—more are to be found.

Now there are a number of returns in which each knight had four sureties, whereas in earlier and later returns for the same county only two sureties are met with. But in these returns each borough representative likewise has four sureties, and, likewise, two sureties at other times.[1]

On this evidence the sheriffs must have required the higher number of sureties for the borough members as well and it is not too bold a generalization that in general the sheriffs decided upon the number of sureties for the borough representatives.

But did the sheriffs only communicate to the bailiffs of the towns how many sureties they were to appoint, or did they themselves undertake this business as they did in the case of the knights of the shire?

Here the names of the sureties and the way in which they recur must be observed.

In a number of cases, one surety guaranteed, in the same return, the appearance of a knight and of a burgess.[2]

A number of sureties guaranteed, in the same return, the ap-

---

[1] E.g. in 1311, 1313, 1318, and at other times, each knight and burgess of Yorkshire had two sureties, but suddenly, on 20 January 1315, everyone had four (*P.W.* ii, ii, 142, 53). Kent, in the years 1290, 1295, 1301, had two sureties for each representative; but on 25 May 1298 four for each knight and burgess (*P.W.* i, 70, 18). Similarly in Hertfordshire, there were two manu-captors for each member in 1295, 1297, 1301, 1302; but in 1298 and 1311 there were four (*P.W.* i, 70; ii, ii, 47).

[2] *P.W.* ii, ii, 201, William de Fevre was surety for a knight of the shire for Yorkshire and for a burgess for Kingston-upon-Hull; *ibid.* 242, William le Bedel, for a knight of Wiltshire and for a citizen of Salisbury; *ibid.* 248, Richard West, for representatives of the county and for the borough of Bedford; *ibid.* 272, Thomas Everard, for a knight and a burgess of Northampton.

pearance of representatives of different boroughs within the same county.[1]

From this it follows that the appointment of the sureties took place in the county court; for otherwise each borough representative would have had only his fellow townsmen as guarantors.

The different towns of the shire were admittedly only very poorly represented in the county court; when the sheriff sought for sureties for the borough representatives, he often enough had to accept mutual guarantees from those elected or the same sureties for both representatives. For this reason, also, it was only in the county court that the same sureties for members of county and borough, or of different boroughs, would be accepted because others could not so immediately be found.[2]

This business, through which the sheriff took over the responsibility for the punctual attendance of the representatives who had been elected in the boroughs, had the important consequence, that the election returns must follow the round-about way through this intermediary, and that the control over the appointment as well as over the summoning of the borough representatives was entirely removed from the purview of the royal chancery.

---

[1] E.g. *P.W.* II, ii, 105, Exeter and Torrington (John atte Weye); *ibid.* 146, Oxford and Witney (John le Baker); *ibid.* 208, Shoreham and Bramber (Robert le Tanner); *ibid.* 222, Plympton and Totnes (John atte Green); *ibid.* 227, Chichester and Midhurst (James de Pittlee).

[2] The most striking example of this is *P.W.* II, ii, 147, 71, Somerset (20 January 1315):

Burgenses Wells:		Burg. de Cherd:	
John de Mertok	{ John Bouedich. { John Auel.	John Bouedich	{ John Mertok. { John Bouedich.
Walter de Legh	{ John Mertok. { John Bouedich.	Thomas Hanel	{ Walter de Legh. { John Bouedich.

Here are four representatives and eight sureties, but altogether only five individuals.

[Riess here makes no allowance for the probability of more than one person having the same name. Since a man could not well be his own surety, it seems clear that there were at least two men named John Bovedich.]

APPENDIX III (TO CHAPTER V)

HOW *the* RIGHT *of the* LOWER HOUSE *to* ASSENT *to* LEGISLA-
TION DEVELOPED *from the* COMMONS' RIGHT *to* PRESENT
PETITIONS

From the beginning it was intended that the commons should not
only serve indirectly as a check on abuses of official power, but should
also bring to the attention of the central government any hardships
that might arise from the due administration of the law. Yet the
members were nothing but the messengers who brought the complaints and petitions from their districts to parliament, and there,
when necessary, gave their opinion or imparted fuller information.

But as early as 14 Edward II the elected members came to confer
together concerning a general grievance, and as a result of their
deliberations presented a common petition to chancery.[1]

Then Edward III adopted the plan of making a distinction in the
petitions. He instructed the commons to deliver the petitions from individuals to the person who formerly received them, the chancellor, but
those touching whole districts to the clerk of the parliament.[2] The
consequence of this was that a special place had to be assigned,[3] where
the commons drew up in proper form the petitions of their constituencies. Thereafter the commons in every parliament had their established meeting-place, and two classes of petitions accumulated, those
that concerned the commons and those that concerned individuals.

It is true that now the petitions that were delivered in the chamber
of the commons usually had the formal beginning, "Item prient les
Communes"—or "la Commune"—but numerous examples show us
that the petitions of the commons, inscribed on the common roll of
parchment, and read over and answered at the end of the parliament,
were by no means all common acts of the whole body of representatives.[4]
We are not yet able to discern in them "motions of the lower

---

[1] *Rot. Parl.* I, 371, 5: "In hoc Parliamento, inter ceteras Petitiones Domino
Regi porrectas, quedam Petitio per Milites, Cives et Burgenses, pro Comita-
tibus, Civitatibus, & Burgis Regni sui ibidem existentes,...."

[2] *Rot. Parl.* II, 201, 4 (22 Edward III): "Et puis fu dit as dites Communes,
que touz les singulers persones qui vourroient liverer Petitions en ce Parlement les ferroient liverer au Chanceller. Et que les Petitions touchantes les
Communes ferroient liverer au Clerc du Parlement."

[3] The first mention of such a place occurs in 25 Edward III.

[4] *Rot. Parl.* III, 45 59: "la Commune des Countees d'Essex et Hertford";
ibid. 46, 64: "les Communes en Countee de Kent"; *ibid.* 47, 72: "les
[Communes] de l'Isle de Wyght"; *ibid.* 63, 38: "Item monstrent les Communes, & nomement les povres Communes del Countee de Cumbr'"; *ibid.* 95,
42; "les Communes du Countee de Derby"; *ibid.* 95,43: "les Communes des
Surrey & Sussex", etc.

house".[1] When the commons really united to make a request and wished to add weight to their petition, they chose for this the form that was long in use for the making of money grants; they came in procession before the king and the barons, and by the mouth of their speaker set forth their petition.[2]

That their assent was asked at times and that they were regularly mentioned in the statutes was, no doubt, on account of the higher "moral authority" which the laws thereby received.[3] But as yet there can be no question of a real constitutional participation of the commons in Legislation; for such participation would imply: 1, that no law should be issued without their express assent; 2, that no law made with their assent should be altered or annulled without their express permission; and 3, that in the drafts of laws which they laid before the king or the upper house nothing should be altered without their assent. But as long as the English kings promulgated statutes by the advice of their *Magnum Concilium*, their power was not limited by the lower house.

Only when Richard II, in agreement with the commons and by overpowering the upper house, imposed taxes and issued laws did the authority of the lower house as a corporation with full equal rights suddenly arise. Out of the commons who had come together an independent determining assembly with established authority was created. Henry IV, and Henry V, recognized in detail and by express regulations what had been won in a half-revolutionary manner during the struggle between Richard II and his barons.

In rapid succession decrees were issued that corresponded to the new position of the lower house.

Henry IV expressly granted to the commons "the right to deliberate and make demands; to consider all matters among themselves that they might, according to their knowledge, bring them to the best end and conclusion".[4] His successor soon added to this the ruling that to announce their decisions they did not require the ceremonious traditional form used for the granting of money, but could employy the procedure of the petitions.[5]

---

[1] Thus the written answers, which in any case were still more specialized than those which were read over, went to the individual members (*Rot. Parl.* II, 316, 7): "...Et fust dit as Communes, Il plest au Roi, que ces qui voleient demurer pur attendre & avoir Respons de lour Petitions,...." This interpretation corresponds also to a decision which Henry IV gave in 1399: "Celuy qui enfourma la Bille viegne au Roy & son Counseill pur luy enfourmer clerement, & le Roy luy ferra remedie", *Rot. Parl.* III, 446, 159.

[2] See especially the "Requests par bouche", *Rot. Parl.* III, 573 ff.

[3] Gneist, *Englische Verfassungsgeschichte*, p. 375, n. 3 a.

[4] *Rot. Parl.* III, 456, 11: "...que mesmes les Communes aient deliberation & advis a communer & traiter toutes leur matires entre eux mesmes, pur la mesner a meillour fyn & conclusion, a leur escience,...".

[5] *Rot. Parl.* IV, 4, 8.

The commons now treated private petitions as requiring their approval, and they themselves accepted petitions.[1] They required a definite answer to each of their motions and would collectively, not merely, as formerly, through commissioners who were present at the discussions of the lords, make binding decrees.[2] They expressly deny to every individual member the right of acting independently for his constituency and of approaching the king and his council. Above all, they demanded the right of assenting to the laws in their entirety as described above.[3] Moreover, they did not omit to obtain from Henry IV the guarantee of a measure of freedom of speech.[4]

In all this the fundamental change that had been brought about under Richard II most clearly appears.[5]

[1] After 1400, the petitions received in the chancery entirely disappear.

[2] *Rot. Parl.* III, 611, 22: "...Et qe par semblable manere bien lise as Communes, de lour part, de comuner ensemble de l'estate et remedie suis dit." That the main emphasis is on the word "ensemble" appears from the context.

[3] See Gneist, *Englische Verfassungsgeschichte*, p. 375.

[4] *Rot. Parl.* III, 466, 46 (2 Henry IV): "...q'en cas q'ils, ou ascun de eux, par ignorance ou negligence soi avoient aucunement mespris en parol ou en fait encontre son Roial Estat, que purroit aucunement tournir a displaisance de sa Roial persone, q'il pleust a mesme nostre Sr̃. le Roi de sa benigne grace leur ent faire pleine grace & pardon. Quele prier le Roy lour ottroia entierment & de bon coer." Thus no absolute freedom of speech.

[5] [For the fullest recent discussion of this matter see H. L. Gray, *The Influence of the Commons on Early Legislation*, and the Critical Memorandum on this work in S. B. Chrimes, *English Constitutional Ideas in the Fifteenth Century*, pp. 236–49. Gray has ignored the important articles by H. G. Richardson and G. O. Sayles on "The King's Ministers in Parliament", *E.H.R.* vols. XLVI, XLVII, showing that the Commons' petitions were often due to the initiative of others.]

The DATE of the COMPOSITION of the "MODUS TENENDI PARLIAMENTUM"

A most remarkable writing is that diminutive treatise which is entitled the *Modus tenendi Parliamentum*; since contemporary sources yield no definite evidence, the date of composition and the significance of this unusual little work have been the subjects of much controversy.

For the scholars of the seventeenth century already saw the impossibility of the statement with which one old manuscript begins: that this is the form and manner of holding a parliament which William the Conqueror had received from Edward the Confessor.

Thus it became necessary to determine to what period the earliest surviving manuscripts of this work belong. Through Hardy's detailed researches[1] it has been ascertained that at least two copies come from the end of the reign of Richard II. Thus the *Modus tenendi Parliamentum* must, at any rate, have been composed before the year 1399.

Since this result did not suffice, an attempt had to be made to discover from the contents a further limitation of the *terminus ante quem*. But in this attempt Hardy has fallen into error in a peculiar way.

For, because among the temporal members of the upper house he found mention only of earls and barons, but not of dukes, he believed that the date of the composition of the interesting work must be pushed back to the time before the first creation of a duke.[2] Similarly, from the statement with regard to expenses, of the maximum amount, five shillings, he draws the conclusion that the *Modus tenendi Parliamentum* must have been written in the time before the daily wage had been regularized and fixed at four shillings. Thus, for two reasons, the year 1327, or the first third of the fourteenth century, appeared to him as the latest date.

But did it at all occur to the author of the *Modus* to enumerate with painful precision and according to heraldic etiquette the dignities whose holders had seats in the upper house? He never indeed mentions the royal princes as a special group; and should he notice the fact that Edward III had made his eldest son Duke of Cornwall, and his younger sons dukes of York and Lancaster? Is it not self-

---

[1] Thomas Duffus Hardy, *Modus tenendi Parliamentum*, Preface.
[2] *Op. cit.* p. viii.

evident that the term earls and barons indicate the lowest limits of the classes privileged by birth and that a raising of the title did not take from any one his status as a baron?

But if the second argument, the statement with regard to the amount of the expenses, is to prove anything as to the date of the work, it must be positively demonstrable that the author had in mind only those rules that were in force or were customary in his own time. But in the absence of legal regulations, might not the highest amount that had ever been reached be set down in order to fix at least a maximum limit? For this is indeed the only purpose of the uncertain expression "infra decem solidos".

Thus the only two pieces of evidence which the careful editor has discovered for determining the date of the remarkable treatise lose for us their importance.

But let us consider the general character of this much discussed work.

In the first place the author's exact familiarity with the internal course of procedure is in a high degree striking. How affairs were to be managed in the absence of the king; and when a baron remains away from the *Magnum Concilium*, how the discussions of the peers (*pares*) proceeded; the police safeguards and measures for keeping order during the parliament; the duties of the usher (*ostiarius*); the accommodation of the special official business; the assignment of the chancery officials to the two houses of the parliament; the formalities of the opening and closing of the sessions—all are described most minutely and with unmistakable certainty.[1] Without doubt the author must have belonged to the royal chancery; this is proved by his knowledge of these numerous external arrangements and the interest he takes in them, and equally by the lively curial style that is reminiscent of the language of the laws.

Thus it is tempting to think of an official work inspired by the king or the representatives of the country, designed to set down in writing the traditional usages of parliament, in order to regulate it. But there is no mention of this purpose, nor was the treatise appealed to in any way during the fourteenth or fifteenth century. Moreover, the number of copies is remarkably small, while other legal regulations were well distributed in England.

May it, then, have been the private work of a chancery official? We will let this question pass for the present, because we still have to bring forward an important piece of evidence for its decision. For more than anything else the tendentious character [*starke Tendenz*] of the *Modus tenendi Parliamentum* is noteworthy.

[1] On this circumstance the English scholars base their assumption of the absolute authenticity of the little work which they treat as a legal document of the first importance. So especially Hardy.

We quote here the most important passages:[1] " . . . and be it known, that when an aid of this kind is to be conceded it is necessary that all the peers of the Parliament consent. And it is to be observed that two knights who come to the parliament for one shire have a greater voice in Parliament in agreeing or dissenting than a great earl of England, and that likewise the clerical representatives of a diocese have a greater voice in Parliament, when they all unite, than the bishop himself, and this is the case in all things, that ought to be granted, refused or done by a Parliament. And from this it is evident that the king can hold a Parliament with the community of his realm without the bishops, earls and barons, provided only that they have been summoned to parliament, though not a single bishop, earl, or baron come in response to the summons; for originally there were no bishops, nor earls, nor barons and yet, at that time, the kings held their Parliaments. But in the other case the opposite is true. The commons (ecclesiastical and lay) may be regularly summoned to Parliament, and if for any reason they will not come, as for example, if they assert that the lord king has not ruled them as he ought and specify in what points, then there would be no parliament at all, even though the archbishops, bishops, earls, and barons and all their peers be present with the king. And therefore it is necessary that all that is to be enforced or repealed, granted or refused, or accomplished, by the Parliament is to be agreed to by the community of the Parliament, which consists of the three estates or classes of Parliament; that is, of the representatives of the clergy, the knights of the shires, the citizens and burgesses, for they represent the whole community of England; and not by the magnates, because each of them appears in parliament for himself and for no one else."

Thus the unknown writer will place the centre of gravity of the parliament in the lower house; only to the assent of the commons is the king bound; alone with them, even without the magnates, the king can unite to form a parliament; when the elected representatives on account of special acts of misgovernment remain away, there is no parliament in the land.

How directly all this contradicts the tradition, the actual usages of parliament! Laws were promulgated, taxes were raised without the commons having given their assent; especially under the first Edwards, numerous parliaments were held when only the earls, barons and bishops were summoned and attended. But our author lays down only the necessity of the summoning of bishops and barons, not the necessity of their attendance.[2]

---

[1] *Modus tenendi Parliamentum*, p. 41: "De auxilio Regis."
[2] Gneist sees in the author an ideologist of feudalism because he asserts the right of a summons for every possessor of thirteen and a third knight's fees as a baron, and for every possessor of twenty knight's fees as an earl.

Indeed what he attributes to the commons can only be taken as a demand. He seeks to support it by the false historical claim that the English kings had held parliaments before there were either earls or barons or bishops: by the doubtful appeal to reason that these lower grades were really representatives of the community of the country, while the magnates acted only for themselves.

How could it happen that the juridical work of a chancery official breathes such hatred against the upper house and attributes to the commons rights that they never claimed, much less exercised? What was the motive for so bold a misrepresentation of the truth on the part of a man who, as we see, was extremely well informed?

In order to clear up this point, we shall have to consider a second obvious invention of this unknown author.

When in a parliament unanimity, or even the agreement of a large majority, is unattainable, a most unusual expedient is to be employed. The three most important court officials, the seneschal, the constable, and the marshall, or two of them, shall choose twenty-five persons from among the members of the parliament, viz. two bishops, two earls, three barons, three representatives of the clergy, five knights of the shire, five citizens and five burgesses.[1] To this commission, which should take decisions instead of the whole parliament, the lower house, then, appointed fifteen members; the upper house, seven; the clergy, three. Of course, this method was never followed,[2] but it is interesting to see for what cases the author of the *Modus tenendi Parliamentum* had provided it, "and if through discord between them, the king and any nobles, or, perhaps, between the magnates themselves, the peace of the realm is disturbed" the remarkable chapter "De Cassibus difficilibus" establishes the need for this extraordinary remedy.

It is, therefore, evident that the *Modus tenendi Parliamentum* must have been composed at a time in which there was bitter strife between the king and the upper house, and in which the power of the lower house was to be strengthened, because in it was seen a faithful ally of the royal cause. Such a combination of circumstances existed, during the last twelve years of Richard II. Since, moreover, the oldest manuscripts go back to that time, there is no objection

---

But obviously that mediaeval writer was not interested in proving the existence of an original division into estates independent of subinfeudation when he made that calculation with his sums. Rather he stated wilfully as the reason for the position of the lords, which seemed to him too exalted, their greater possession which was the most insufficient title.

[1] For so the twenty-five persons were to be made up. *Modus tenendi Parliamentum*, p. 19: "De Cassibus et Judiciis difficilibus."

[2] [There is, however, a striking similarity between this committee and that sent to Kenilworth in 1327 to renounce allegiance to Edward II. M. V. Clarke, *Mediaeval Representation and Consent*, chapter IX.]

against the assumption of its having been written during that period.

Probably the king himself suggested the composition of this work. It should be effective for the moment when the opposing upper house would bring its legal claims determinedly into force, and, by the laws, frustrate every governmertt. Then this tendentious codification of the rights of parliament could be brought forward and the last resistance of the barons suppressed by the appearance of ancient enumerated rights which had, in practice, been obscured only through abuses.

But the taking of this well-prepared step was prevented by the return of the banished Duke of Lancaster and the sudden change to methods of force.

The defeat which led Richard II to the prison of the Tower also consigned this relic of his *coup d'état* for a long time to come to the darkness of the royal archives.[1]

---

[1] [Riess's theory of the origin of the *Modus tenendi Parliamentum* has never been accepted, and since his time several different opinions as to its date have been advanced. M. Bémont, who was the first scholar to attempt a systematic survey of the manuscripts ("La Date de la Composition du Modus Tenendi Parliamentum in Anglia", *Mélanges Julien Havet*, pp. 465–80), concluded that it was written soon after 1377. Professor Tout "inclined to the view that it was drawn up not before 1340 but probably not very long afterwards" (*Chapters in English Administrative History*, III, 139). The two most recent writers on the subject, Professor W. A. Morris ("The Date of the *Modus Tenendi Parliamentum*", *E.H.R.* XLIX, 407–22) and the late Miss M. V. Clarke (*Mediaeval Representation and Consent*), have advanced weighty arguments in favour of the view that it belongs to the later years of the reign of Edward II.]

AUTHORITIES CITED

Alexander, J. J. The Dates of County Days. (Bulletin of the Inst. of Hist. Research, III, 89–95.)

— Devon County Members of Parliament. (Reports and Trans. of the Devonshire Association, XLV, 247–69.)

Bémont, C. La Date de la Composition du Modus Tenendi Parliamentum in Anglia. (Mélanges Julien Havet, pp. 465–80. Paris, 1895.)

Britton. Treatise of Law. Ed. F. M. Nichols. 2 vols. Oxford, 1865.

Calendar of Close Rolls, 1313–18. London, 1893.

Calendar of Fine Rolls, VI, VIII. London, 1921, 1924.

Calendar of Inquisitions post mortem, II. London, 1906.

Cam, H. M. The Hundred and the Hundred Rolls. London, 1930.

Chrimes, S. B. English Constitutional Ideas in the Fifteenth Century. Cambridge, 1936.

Clarke, M. V. Mediaeval Representation and Consent. London, 1936.

Cox, H. Antient Parliamentary Elections. London, 1868.

Dickinson, W. C. County Days in Scotland. (Bulletin of the Inst. of Hist. Research, III, 161–7.)

Edwards, J. G. The Personnel of the Commons in Parliament under Edward I and Edward II. (Essays in Medieval History presented to Thomas Frederick Tout, No. 16. Manchester, 1925.)

— The Plena Potestas of English Parliamentary Representatives. (Oxford Essays in Medieval History presented to Herbert Edward Salter, pp. 141–54. Oxford, 1934.)

Gneist, R. Geschichte und heutige Gestalt der englischen Communalverfassung oder des Selfgovernment. 2 vols. Berlin, 1863.

— Englische Verfassungsgeschichte. Berlin, 1882.

— — (Translated into English by P. A. Ashworth. London, 1891.)

Gray, H. L. The Influence of the Commons on Early Legislation. Cambridge, Mass., 1932.

Hallam, H. Constitutional History of England. (Chandos Classics edition. 1873.)

Jolliffe, J. E. A. The Constitutional History of Medieval England from the English Settlement to 1485. London, 1937.

Latham, L. C. The Collection of the Wages of the Knights of the Shire in the 14th and 15th Centuries. (E.H.R. XLVIII, 455–64.)

Leicht, P. S. Un principio politico medioevale. (Reale Accademia nazionale dei Lincei, Rendiconte, XXIX, 232 ff.)

Lobel, M. D. The Borough of Bury St Edmund's. Oxford, 1935.

Maitland, F. W. The Constitutional History of England. Cambridge, 1908.

May, Sir T. E. A Treatise on the Law, Privileges, Proceedings, and Usage of Parliament. 4th edition. London, 1859. (Cited as "Parliamentary Practice".)

McIlwain, C. H. The High Court of Parliament. New Haven, 1910.
— Medieval Estates. (Cambridge Medieval History, VII, 665–715. Cambridge, 1932.)
McKisack, M. The Parliamentary Representation of the English Boroughs during the Middle Ages. Oxford, 1932.
Merewether, H. A. and A. J. Stephens. The History of the Boroughs and Municipal Corporations of the United Kingdom from the earliest to the present time, I. London, 1835.
Modus Tenendi Parliamentum. Ed. Sir T. D. Hardy. (R.C.) London, 1843.
Morris, W. A. The Early English County Court. Berkeley, Cal., 1926.
— The Medieval English Sheriff to 1300. Manchester, 1927.
— The Date of the Modus Tenendi Parliamentum. (E.H.R. XLIX, 407–22.)
Noorden, C. v. Zur Geschichte und Literatur des englischen Self-government. (Historische Zeitschrift, XIII, 1–89.)
Parliamentary Writs. Ed. Sir F. Palgrave. 2 vols. in 4. (R.C.) London, 1827–34.
Pasquet, D. An Essay on the Origin of the House of Commons. Translated into English by R. G. D. Laffan with a Preface and Additional Notes by G. T. Lapsley. Cambridge, 1925.
Paston Letters, with Notes by John Fenn. 5 vols. London, 1783–1823.
Pollard, A. F. The Evolution of Parliament. 2nd ed. London, 1926.
Pollock, Sir F. and F. W. Maitland. The History of English Law before the time of Edward I. 2nd ed. Cambridge, 1898.
Prynne, W. Brevia Parliamentaria Rediviva. London, 1662.
Reports from the Lords' Committees...touching the Dignity of a Peer. 5 vols. London, 1820–9.
Return of Members of Parliament, 1213–1702. London, 1879.
Richardson, H. G. and G. O. Sayles. The King's Ministers in Parliament, 1272–1377. (E.H.R. XLVI, 529–50; XLVII, 194–203, 377–97.)
Rotuli Parliamentorum. Ed. J. Strachey and others. 6 vols. London, 1767–77.
Rymer, T. Foedera. Hague edition, 1737–45.
Statutes of the Realm, I, II. (R.C.) London, 1810, 1816.
Stephenson, Carl. Taxation and Representation in the Middle Ages. (Anniversary Essays in Medieval History by students of C. H. Haskins, pp. 291–312. Boston, Mass., 1929.)
Stubbs, W. Constitutional History of England. 3 vols. Oxford, 1874–8.
— Select Charters and other illustrations of English Constitutional History. Oxford, 1870.
Tait, J. The Medieval English Borough. Manchester, 1936.
Tout, T. F. Chapters in the Administrative History of Medieval England, IV. Manchester, 1928.
Trenholme, N. M. The English Monastic Boroughs. Columbia, Missouri, 1927.

Wilkinson, B. Studies in the Constitutional History of the Thirteenth and Fourteenth Centuries. Manchester, 1937.

Willard, J. F. Parliamentary Taxes on Personal Property, 1290–1334. Cambridge, Mass., 1934.

— Taxation Boroughs and Parliamentary Boroughs. (Historial Essays in honour of James Tait. Manchester, 1933.)

Wood-Legh, K. L. The Knights' Attendance in the Parliaments of Edward III. (E.H.R. XLVII, 398–413.)

— Sheriffs, Lawyers and Belted Knights in the Parliaments of Edward III. (E.H.R. XLVI, 372–88.)

INDEX

CAMBRIDGE: PRINTED BY W. LEWIS, M.A., AT THE UNIVERSITY PRESS

For EU product safety concerns, contact us at Calle de José Abascal, 56–1°, 28003 Madrid, Spain or eugpsr@cambridge.org.